Smart High School Series

Number Sense and Algebra

ISBN: 978-1-77149-360-4

Printed in China

Smart High School Series – MathSmart Grade 9 (Number Sense and Algebra) is designed to help students build solid foundations in high-school-level math and excel in key math concepts.

This workbook covers the key concepts of number sense and algebra in the Mathematics curriculum, including topics on:

- Laws of Exponents
- Operations with Polynomials
- Algebraic Expressions and Equations

This workbook contains four chapters, with each chapter covering a math topic. Different concepts within the topic are each introduced by a "Key Ideas" section and examples are provided to give students an opportunity to consolidate their understanding. The "Try these!" section allows students to ease into the concept with basic skill questions, and is followed by the "Practice" section with questions that gradually increase in difficulty to help students consolidate the concept they have learned. Useful hints are provided to guide students along and help them grasp the essential math concepts. In addition, a handy summary of the concepts learned is included at the end of each chapter along with space for students to make their own notes for quick and easy reference whenever needed.

A quiz at the end of each chapter as well as a final test are provided to recapitulate the concepts and skills students have learned in the book. The questions are classified into four categories to help students evaluate their own learning. Below are the four categories:

- Knowledge and Understanding
- Application
- Communication
- Thinking

This approach to testing practice effectively prepares students for the Math examination in school.

Additionally, the "Math IRL" sections throughout the book demonstrate the use of the investigated math topics in real-life scenarios to help students recognize the ubiquity and function of math in everyday settings. Bonus online resources can also be accessed by scanning the included QR codes.

At the end of this workbook is an answer key that provides thorough solutions with the crucial steps clearly presented to help students develop an understanding of the correct strategies and approaches to arrive at the solutions.

MathSmart Grade 9 (Number Sense and Algebra) will undoubtedly reinforce students' math skills and strengthen the conceptual foundation needed as a prerequisite for exploring mathematics further in their secondary programs.

Contents

Numeracy

1.1 Integers

Key Ideas

Integers are all positive and negative whole numbers, including zero. Some rules, such as BEDMAS, must be followed when doing operations on integers.

To use a number line for adding or subtracting integers, take the first number in an expression as the starting point and move the correct number of units to the right or to the left to find the answer.

Adding or Subtracting Integers

adding a positive integer
OR
subtracting a negative integer
➤ Move the units to the right.

adding a negative integer
OR
subtracting a positive integer
➤ Move the units to the left.

Examples

move right
$-3 + (+2) = -1$
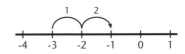

move right
$-3 - (-2) = -1$
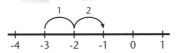

move left
$-3 + (-2) = -5$
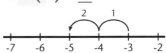

move left
$-3 - (+2) = -5$

Trace the correct arrows to show in which direction the units should move. Then find the answers.

Try these!

① $5 + (-2) =$

move
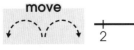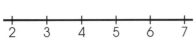

② $-1 - (+3) =$

move
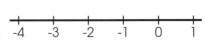

③ $-4 + (+1) =$

move
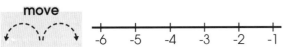

④ $-2 - (-2) =$

move
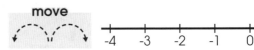

Do the addition and subtraction. Show your steps.

⑤   5 + (-2)

= 5 ⬚ 2

= ⬚

⑥   10 – (+3)

= 10 ⬚ 3

= ⬚

⑦   7 – (-2)

= 7 ⬚ 2

= ⬚

⑧   (-9) – (+5)

⑨   (+2) + (-8)

⑩   (-4) + (-5)

⑪   (-3) + (+1)

⑫   (-5) – (-8)

⑬   (-7) – (+10)

Hint

Adding a positive number or subtracting a negative number is an addition.

e.g. 4 + (+3) = 4 + 3
       4 – (-3) = 4 + 3

Adding a negative number or subtracting a positive number is a subtraction.

e.g. 4 + (-3) = 4 – 3
       4 – (+3) = 4 – 3

Add "+" or "–" for each answer.

⑭   (+7) × (+2) = ⬚ 14

⑮   (-9) ÷ (-3) = ⬚ 3

⑯   (+10) ÷ (-5) = ⬚ 2

⑰   (-5) × (-2) = ⬚ 10

⑱   (+8) ÷ (+2) = ⬚ 4

⑲   (-16) ÷ (-4) = ⬚ 4

⑳   (-2) × (+3) = ⬚ 6

㉑   (+4) × (-3) = ⬚ 12

Hint

In multiplication and division, same signs yield a positive answer; different signs yield a negative answer.

Same Signs:
(+) × (+)
(–) × (–)
(+) ÷ (+)   ➡   (+)
(–) ÷ (–)

Different Signs:
(+) × (–)
(–) × (+)
(+) ÷ (–)   ➡   (–)
(–) ÷ (+)

Do the multiplication and division.

㉒   (+3) × (-3)   = _____

㉓   (-5) × (-6)   = _____

㉔   (+24) ÷ (-8) = _____

㉕   (-30) ÷ (+2) = _____

㉖   (+6) × (+7)   = _____

㉗   (-9) × (+3)   = _____

㉘   (-32) ÷ (-4) = _____

㉙   (+35) ÷ (-5) = _____

㉚   (-5) × (-7)   = _____

㉛   (+63) ÷ (-9) = _____

㉜   (-32) ÷ (+4) = _____

㉝   (-45) ÷ (-3) = _____

Evaluate each expression. Show your work.

㉞ $(-2) + (-5) \times (-4)$

$= (-2) + (\underline{\hspace{2cm}})$

$= \underline{\hspace{1.5cm}}$

㉟ $(+5) - (-15) \div (+3)$

Hint

Remember BEDMAS to follow the order of operations.

Brackets
Exponents
Division/**M**ultiplication
Addition/**S**ubtraction

㊱ $(-16) \div (+4) - (-8)$

㊲ $((-6) + 2) \div (-4)$

㊳ $(-10) + 3^2 \times 2$

㊴ $(5 - 3^2) \div (-2)$

㊵ $((-9) + 12)^2 - 4$

㊶ $1 + (5 + (-3))^2 - 12$

㊷ $((-1) \times 4^2) - (-16)$

㊸ $((6 - (-5)) + (-7))^2$

㊹ $((-2)^2 - 5) \times ((-4) - 7)$

㊺ $((-1) + 9) \div ((-2) + 2^2)$

㊻ $((-1) + 4 \div 2)^2 \times ((-12) \div 4)^2$

㊼ $((-4) - (-9))^2 \div (2^2 - 3^2)$

Evaluate each expression.

(48) a. $(+30) \div (-6) - (-7)$ b. $(+4) \div (-2) \times (-3)$

c. $(-20) - (-4) \times (+5)$ d. $(-15) + (-6) - (-5)$

e. $((-11) + (-3)) \div (-7)$ f. $(-40) \times (-2) \div (-4)$

g. $18 + (-4 \times 3) + (-2)$ h. $16 - (-4) \times 5 + 9$

(49) a. $3^2 \times (-2) + 6$ b. $(-5) \times 2^2 + (-2)$

c. $17 - (-9) - (-3)^2$ d. $(-13) - 4^2 + (-5)$

e. $(-29) + 6^2 \div (-3)$ f. $3^2 + 5 \times (-2) \div (-1)$

g. $5^2 + (-9) \times 3$ h. $12 - (-2^2) \times 6 + 4$

(50) a. $(3^2 - 2) \times (2^2 - 9)$ b. $(-11) \times 5 + (4^2 - 3)$

c. $(5 \times (-4) - 2) + 3^2$ d. $((-4) - (-7))^2 \div (2^2 - 1)$

e. $(4^2 - 3^2)^2 \times (9 - 12)$ f. $(-3) \times (-6) \div ((-6) + 9)^2$

g. $(8 + (-2))^2 + ((-2) + (-5))^2$ h. $(3^2 \times 2 + 3) - ((-20) \div 5)^2$

Answer the questions.

(51) Give examples of two types of numbers that are not integers.

(52) Without evaluating, determine if the expression $((-4) \times (-8))^2$ will yield a positive or negative number. Explain your reasoning.

(53) Without evaluating, determine which expression is greater, $(8 \times (-4))^2$ or $8^2 \times (-4)$? Explain your reasoning.

(54) If the product of a positive integer and an unknown is a negative integer, is the unknown a positive or negative integer?

(55) A share of GoBiz stock was worth \$15 on Monday. The stock fell by \$3 on Tuesday and rose by \$1 on Wednesday. Sarah bought 10 shares on Monday and sold them on Wednesday. What was the net profit?

(56) Last week, there were 3 days at 5°C, 2 days at -3°C, and 2 days at -8°C. What was the average daily temperature?

Chapter 1

1.2 Rational Numbers and Irrational Numbers

Key Ideas

A rational number is a number that can be expressed as a fraction of two integers, where the denominator cannot be zero.

$$\text{rational number} = \frac{p}{q},$$

where p and q are integers and $p \neq 0$

If a number cannot be expressed as a fraction of two integers, where the denominator is not zero, then it is not a rational number. Numbers that are not rational are called irrational numbers.

Examples

Rational Numbers:

$2 \left(= \frac{2}{1} \right)$ $-3 \left(= \frac{-3}{1} \right)$

$0.1 \left(= \frac{1}{10} \right)$ $1.7 \left(= \frac{17}{10} \right)$

$0.\overline{3} \left(= \frac{1}{3} \right)$ $-1.09 \left(= \frac{-109}{100} \right)$

$1\frac{2}{3} \left(= \frac{5}{3} \right)$ $\sqrt{16} \left(= \frac{4}{1} \right)$

Irrational Numbers:

π

$\sqrt{2}$

cannot be expressed as a fraction of two integers

Write each number as a fraction of two integers if possible. Write "R" for rational and "I" for irrational numbers in the circles.

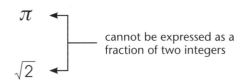

Try these!

① ◯ $3 = \dfrac{\quad}{1}$

② ◯ $-8 = \dfrac{\quad}{\quad}$

③ ◯ $\sqrt{10} = \dfrac{\quad}{\quad}$

④ ◯ $0 = \dfrac{\quad}{\quad}$

⑤ ◯ $0.7 = \dfrac{\quad}{\quad}$

⑥ ◯ $0.21 = \dfrac{\quad}{\quad}$

⑦ ◯ $\dfrac{1}{\sqrt{3}} = \dfrac{\quad}{\quad}$

⑧ ◯ $1\frac{1}{3} = \dfrac{\quad}{\quad}$

⑨ ◯ $-1.9 = \dfrac{\quad}{\quad}$

⑩ ◯ $-1\frac{1}{4} = \dfrac{\quad}{\quad}$

⑪ ◯ $\dfrac{5}{\sqrt{2}} = \dfrac{\quad}{\quad}$

⑫ ◯ $-0.01 = \dfrac{\quad}{\quad}$

Circle the rational numbers. Rewrite each rational number as a fraction of two integers beside it. Then answer the questions.

⑬ a. 5

b. $1\dfrac{3}{5}$

c. -0.8

d. $\sqrt{9}$

e. $-2\dfrac{1}{2}$

f. -9

g. $\dfrac{1}{\sqrt{7}}$

h. 1.15

i. 3.01

j. $-\sqrt{11}$

k. $(-3)^2$

l. -1.009

m. 2^2

n. $-\dfrac{4}{\sqrt{4}}$

o. $\dfrac{2.2}{2}$

p. $\dfrac{0}{1^2}$

⑭ Consider all the rational numbers above. List the rational numbers that are

a. smaller than -1. _____

b. greater than 3. _____

c. between -1 and 3. _____

Add or subtract the rational numbers. Write the answers as fractions.

⑮ $\dfrac{1}{3} + \dfrac{1}{4}$

⑯ $\dfrac{4}{5} - \dfrac{1}{2}$

⑰ $-\dfrac{2}{3} + 1\dfrac{3}{4}$

Hint

Convert the numbers to common forms in either fractions or decimals before doing the calculations.

⑱ $\dfrac{1}{5} + (-\dfrac{5}{6})$

⑲ $-\dfrac{3}{4} - \dfrac{1}{8}$

⑳ $\dfrac{7}{10} - \dfrac{3}{4}$

㉑ $2.3 + 1\dfrac{1}{5}$

㉒ $4.5 - 2\dfrac{2}{5}$

㉓ $\dfrac{1}{6} - 0.7$

㉔ $2.05 + (-\dfrac{9}{20})$

Multiply and divide the rational numbers. Write the answers as fractions.

㉕ $\dfrac{1}{4} \times \dfrac{1}{3}$

㉖ $\dfrac{2}{5} \times (-\dfrac{1}{3})$

㉗ $\dfrac{5}{8} \times (-\dfrac{3}{5})$

㉘ $-2\dfrac{4}{5} \times 1\dfrac{3}{7}$

㉙ $3^2 \div \dfrac{1}{3}$

㉚ $10 \div \dfrac{3}{4}$

㉛ $-3\dfrac{3}{4} \times \sqrt{16}$

㉜ $\dfrac{7}{8} \div (-0.5)$

㉝ $1\dfrac{1}{2} \times 2.5$

㉞ -2.25×10^2

㉟ $2.5 \div \dfrac{5}{2^2}$

㊱ $-3.2 \div (-\dfrac{2^3}{3^2})$

Evaluate each expression.

㊲ $-\dfrac{2}{3} \times \dfrac{5}{6} + \dfrac{1}{3}$

㊳ $-\sqrt{9} - 2\dfrac{4}{5} \times 1\dfrac{3}{7}$

㊴ $14 \div (\dfrac{1}{2} - (-1.25))$

㊵ $-\dfrac{1}{\sqrt{9}} + 1\dfrac{7}{9} \div (-\dfrac{4}{3})$

㊶ $0.4 \div (-\dfrac{6}{5}) + \dfrac{1}{3}$

㊷ $-1\dfrac{2}{7} \times \dfrac{8}{3} - (-\dfrac{2^2}{7})$

㊸ $-\dfrac{15}{8} \times \dfrac{\sqrt{36}}{5} + 0.25$

㊹ $(-\dfrac{6}{7}) \div (-\dfrac{2^3}{14}) + \dfrac{1}{2}$

㊺ $(0.5 - \dfrac{3}{4}) \times (\dfrac{15}{2^2} \div (-\dfrac{3^2}{8}))$

Answer the questions.

㊻ Consider each set of numbers below.

Set A: $\dfrac{1}{7}, \dfrac{0}{9}, -\dfrac{3}{4}, \dfrac{\sqrt{9}}{3}, \dfrac{9}{\sqrt{3}}, -\dfrac{14}{8}, 1\dfrac{5}{9}$

Set B: -9, 0.35, -2.5, 5.2, $\sqrt{13}$, 0, $-\sqrt{4}$

Set C: 0.55, $-\dfrac{2}{9}$, 3π, $\dfrac{4}{15}$, -5.11, 2.08, $\dfrac{13}{7}$

a. Identify the rational numbers in each set.

b. List the rational numbers in each set in order from smallest to greatest.

㊼ Determine whether each statement below is true or false. Justify your answers.

Hint

A terminating decimal is a decimal that ends.

e.g. 0.5, 1.08

a. All integers are rational numbers.

b. All terminating decimals are rational numbers.

c. The square root of a number is always an irrational number.

d. $\dfrac{1}{3}$ is an irrational number because it is not a terminating decimal ($\dfrac{1}{3} = 0.333...$).

㊽ Dina buys $4\dfrac{1}{5}$ m of rope for $2.50/m and $2\dfrac{2}{3}$ m of lace trimming for $11.25/m. What is the total cost?

㊾ Tamara practised yoga for $3\dfrac{1}{2}$ h last week and $1\dfrac{1}{4}$ h less this week. How many hours did she practise yoga weekly on average?

㊿ Kenny mixed $2\dfrac{2}{5}$ L of orange juice, 3.3 L of apple juice, and $1\dfrac{1}{2}$ L of cranberry juice to make fruit punch. He then poured the fruit punch equally into 0.6-L cups. How many cups of fruit punch did he make?

M A T H   I R L

For a long time in history, ancient Greek mathematicians believed that all numbers can be expressed as a ratio of whole numbers. However, one mathematician named Hippasus had a different opinion about this concept as he discovered that some numbers cannot be expressed as ratios of whole numbers, which we now call irrational numbers. Unfortunately, Hippasus's discovery was not well received at that time and legend says that he suffered dire consequences as a result. Today, we know not only that irrational numbers exist but also that they play an important role in mathematics. Scan the QR code to learn about some famous irrational numbers.

Chapter 1

1.3   Ratio, Rate, and Proportion

Key Ideas

Ratio, rate, and proportion are used to express mathematical relationships and are applicable in many real-life scenarios.

ratio – a comparison of two quantities with the same unit of measure; can be expressed in fraction form

rate – a comparison of two quantities with different units of measure; unit rate is commonly used where the denominator is 1

proportion – an equation of two equal ratios, commonly expressed in fraction form

Examples

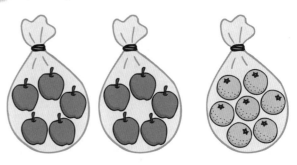

Ratio:

apples to oranges: 10:7 or $\dfrac{10}{7}$

Rate:

10 apples in 2 bags: 10 apples/2 bags

Proportion:

$\dfrac{\text{apples}}{\text{oranges}} = \dfrac{10}{7} = \dfrac{20}{14}$ There are 20 apples for 14 oranges.

Fill in the blanks using the information in the tables. Write the answers in simplest form.

Try these!

①

	Stool	Chair
Room A	5	3
Room B	4	7

a. Room A
- stools to chairs: 5:☐
- chairs to stools: ☐:☐
- all to chairs: ☐:☐

b. Room B
- chairs to stools: 7:☐
- stools to chairs: ☐:☐
- chairs to all: ☐:☐

②

	Circle	Square
Design A	4	6
Design B	8	10

a. Design A   simplest form ↓
- circles to squares: ☐:3
- squares to circles: ☐:☐
- circles to all: ☐:☐

b. Design B   simplest form ↓
- squares to circles: ☐:4
- circles to squares: ☐:☐
- squares to all: ☐:☐

③

	Cookie	Brownie
Jar A	10	12
Jar B	12	12

a. cookies in Jar A to cookies in Jar B: ☐:☐

b. brownies in Jar B to brownies in Jar A: ☐:☐

c. all cookies to all brownies: ☐:☐

Complete the equivalent ratios.

④ 1:2 = 3: _____

⑤ 3:4 = 9: _____

⑥ 2:5 = _____ :10

⑦ 4:2 = 2: _____

⑧ 5:6 = 15: _____

⑨ 9:6 = _____ :2

⑩ 2:8 = _____ :4

⑪ 6:4 = 3: _____

⑫ 7:3 = 21: _____

⑬ 16:4 = _____ :2

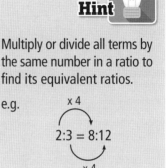

Hint

Multiply or divide all terms by the same number in a ratio to find its equivalent ratios.

e.g.   x 4

2:3 = 8:12

x 4

For each group, find the unit rate. Then use the unit rate to find the answers.

⑭ 18 cookies in 3 packages   **unit rate** _____ cookies/package

   a. Find the number of cookies.

     • 4 packages   • 8 packages

     _____   _____

   b. Find the number of packages.

     • 24 cookies   • 12 cookies

     _____   _____

Hint

A unit rate is simply a rate that has a second term that is 1 unit.

e.g.   10 L in 2 pails

rate: 10 L/2 pails

unit rate: 5 L/pail

↑   ↑

10 ÷ 2 = 5   1 pail

⑮ 80 km in 4 h

unit rate

_____ ← also referred to as speed

   a. Find the distance.

     • 2 h   _____

     • 5 h   _____

     • 8 h   _____

   b. Find the time.

     • 60 km   _____

     • 20 km   _____

     • 30 km   _____

⑯ $120 for 5 shirts

unit rate

_____ ← also referred to as unit price

   a. Find the cost.

     • 2 shirts   _____

     • 6 shirts   _____

     • 13 shirts _____

   b. Find the number of shirts.

     • $96   _____

     • $72   _____

     • $216   _____

Solve the proportions. Show your work.

⑰ $\dfrac{3}{4} = \dfrac{x}{16}$

⑱ $\dfrac{2}{5} = \dfrac{10}{x}$

Hint

Use cross-multiplication to solve proportions.

$$\dfrac{a}{b} \diagup\!\!\!\!\diagdown \dfrac{c}{d}$$

$a \times d = b \times c$

e.g.

$$\dfrac{3}{4} \diagup\!\!\!\!\diagdown \dfrac{12}{x}$$ ← cross-multiply

$3x = 4 \times 12$

$x = 16$

⑲ $\dfrac{x}{8} = \dfrac{3}{2}$

⑳ $\dfrac{7}{x} = \dfrac{21}{33}$

㉑ $\dfrac{10}{7} = \dfrac{7}{x}$

㉒ $\dfrac{5}{4} = \dfrac{x}{10}$

㉓ $\dfrac{x}{3} = \dfrac{12}{25}$

㉔ $\dfrac{18}{x} = \dfrac{10}{3}$

㉕ $\dfrac{5}{4} = \dfrac{21}{x}$

㉖ $\dfrac{1.2}{x} = \dfrac{6}{5}$

Set up a proportion to find each percent or fraction.

Hint

Percent can be considered as a ratio, where the second term is 100.

㉗ $\dfrac{3}{5} = $ _____ %

$\dfrac{3}{5} = \dfrac{x}{100}$

㉘ $\dfrac{1}{4} = $ _____ %

㉙ $\dfrac{29}{50} = $ _____ %

㉚ $26\% = \dfrac{}{50}$

㉛ $45\% = \dfrac{}{20}$

Answer the questions.

③② There are red balls and green balls in a box. The ratio of red balls to green balls is 3:4.

    a. How many red balls are there if there are 24 green balls?

    b. How many green balls are there if there are 45 red balls?

    c. How many red balls and green balls are there if there is a total of 49 balls?

    d. Is it possible to have a total of 60 red balls and green balls? Explain.

③③ Tommy reads 4 books in 2 weeks and Jeff reads 2 books in 6 days. Who reads faster?

③④ It takes Garrett 25 minutes to type 1000 words. If he wants to achieve a typing speed of 50 words/minute, how many more words does he need to type in 25 minutes?

③⑤ For 5 servings, a recipe calls for 3 cups of pancake mix, 2 eggs, and $\frac{1}{2}$ cup of milk. Find how much of each ingredient is needed for the servings.

    a. 10 servings

    b. 12 servings

③⑥ Jenna got 85% on both her English quiz and Math quiz.

    a. If there were 20 questions on the English quiz, how many questions did she answer correctly?

    b. If she answered 9 questions on the Math quiz incorrectly, how many questions were there on the Math quiz?

    c. If Jenna answered 1 more question correctly on each quiz, on which quiz would she have a better score than the other quiz?

③⑦ A home renovation project consists of an upstairs project and a downstairs project. The upstairs project is completed at a rate of 5% per day, while the downstairs project takes a week to complete 14%. When one of the projects is completed, what percent of the other project will remain?

Things I have learned in this chapter:

- performing operations on positive and negative integers
- distinguishing between rational and irrational numbers
- performing operations on rational numbers
- expressing mathematical relationships in ratios, rates, and proportions

My Notes:

_____

_____

_____

_____

_____

_____

_____

_____

_____

Chapter 1

Knowledge and Understanding

Circle the correct answers.

① Which category does the number -3 not belong?

    A. negative number   B. integer

    C. rational number   D. irrational number

② Which of the following is not equivalent to the others?

    A. 2.5%   B. 0.25

    C. $\dfrac{1}{4}$ D. $\dfrac{25}{100}$

③ Which of the following is not a rational number?

    A. $\dfrac{5}{0}$ B. $2\dfrac{1}{7}$

    C. -1.9   D. $\sqrt{0}$

④ What is a comparison of two quantities with different units of measure?

    A. percent   B. ratio

    C. rate   D. proportion

⑤ Which of the following always results in a negative number?

    A. positive number + negative number

    B. positive number − negative number

    C. negative number ÷ positive number

    D. negative number x negative number

⑥ Which part of $(-10) - (3 + 5)^2 \times 4^2$ should be evaluated first?

    A. $(-10) - 3$ B. $(-10) - (3 + 5)^2$

    C. $5^2 \times 4^2$ D. $(3 + 5)$

⑦ Which of the following ratios is not equivalent to the others?

    A. 8:10   B. 4:6

    C. 2:3   D. 1:1.5

Evaluate. Show your work.

⑧ (-9) x (-2)

⑨ $4^2 - (-3)$

⑩ 12 + (-7)

⑪ (-8) ÷ 2 + (-9)

⑫ $(-10) \div (-5) + 2^2$

⑬ $(-3 + 4) \times 3^2$

⑭ $5^2 - 3^2 \times 2^2$

⑮ $(-4)^2 \times (-5) - (-2)$

⑯ $((-3) - (-5)) \times 2^2$

Evaluate each expression. Write the answer as a fraction.

⑰ $3\frac{1}{2} - \frac{5}{8}$

⑱ $4\frac{1}{3} + (-\frac{1}{4})$

⑲ $-\frac{5}{9} \times (-\frac{3}{10})$

⑳ $-\frac{7}{20} \div 2\frac{4}{5}$

㉑ $-3\frac{2}{5} \div 0.2$

㉒ $4.5 \div (-2\frac{1}{4})$

㉓ $(-1.3) \times 1\frac{1}{2} \div \frac{1}{\sqrt{25}}$

㉔ $0.75 \div 2\frac{1}{2} + (-\frac{3}{2})$

㉕ $4^2 - (-\frac{4}{5}) \times 0.5$

㉖ $(\frac{1}{2} + (-\frac{3}{4})) \times (\sqrt{36} - 0.5)$

㉗ $(-1\frac{3}{10}) \times 2\frac{1}{2} \times (-2)^2$

㉘ $(1\frac{3}{5} - 2.1) \times (-2 + 3)^2$

Find the ratios using the information from the tables. Write the answers in simplest form.

㉙

	Tree	Shrub
Garden A	20	12
Garden B	18	16

a. trees to shrubs in Garden A

_____

b. shrubs to trees in Garden B

_____

c. all trees to all shrubs

_____

㉚

	Apple	Orange	Pear
Basket A	8	4	2
Basket B	6	8	5

a. apples to oranges to pears in Basket A

_____

b. oranges to apples to pears in Basket B

_____

c. apples in Basket A to apples in Basket B

_____

Complete the equivalent ratios.

㉛ $3:4 = 6:$ _____

㉜ $5:2 = 15:$ _____

㉝ $6:9 =$ _____ $:3$

㉞ $8:6 =$ _____ $:12$

㉟ $10:5 = 5:$ _____

㊱ $2:8 = 1:$ _____

㊲ $1:7 = 7:$ _____

㊳ $5:4 =$ _____ $:20$

㊴ $12:20 = 3:$ _____

Find the unit rates.

㊵ 60 oranges in 5 bags

_____

㊶ 30 km in 5 h

_____

㊷ $27 for 9 cans

_____

㊸ 24 muffins in 6 boxes

_____

㊹ 50 m in 4 min

_____

㊺ $29 for 4 cartons

_____

Solve for x in each proportion. Show your work.

㊻ $\frac{3}{5} = \frac{9}{x}$

㊼ $\frac{7}{5} = \frac{x}{15}$

㊽ $\frac{x}{8} = \frac{15}{4}$

㊾ $\frac{10}{x} = \frac{4}{5}$

㊿ $\frac{x}{3} = \frac{-4}{12}$

(51) $\frac{7}{2} = \frac{x}{-6}$

(52) $5:6 = 2:x$

(53) $x:5 = 3:4$

(54) $3:x = 2:5$

Application

Solve the problems. Show your work.

(55) Rita purchased 3 books and 2 candles. Each book cost \$12.50 and each candle cost \$9.25. If the sales tax was 13%, what was her change if she paid \$70?

(56) Store A sells 6 mason jars for \$19.20 and Store B sells the same mason jars at \$15 for 4. Find the unit prices. Which store offers a better buy?

57. The table below shows the temperatures recorded in one week in November.

A Week's Temperatures in November

Day	Sun	Mon	Tue	Wed	Thu	Fri	Sat
Temperature	-3°C	-4°C	-11°C	9°C	-2°C	10°C	-6°C

a. What was the daily average temperature?

b. If the following Sunday's temperature was twice of Saturday's temperature, what was the difference in temperature of the two Sundays?

58. On a map, a rectangular park has the dimensions of 6 cm by 4 cm. If the actual measure of one of the park's sides is 30 m, what are the possible areas?

59. A cleaning solution requires the ratio of water to alcohol to be 3:8. A 2-L solution already has 80% alcohol. How much more water needs to be added to this solution to make the cleaning solution?

Communication

Answer the questions.

⑥⓪ Consider each expression. List the ranges of value of a in which the expression would yield a positive answer.

$-5 + a$

$-5 - a$

⑥① Explain why all terminating decimals are rational numbers.

⑥② Is there any integer that when squared is a negative number? Explain.

Thinking

Answer the questions.

⑥③ Solve for x.

a. $\frac{0.6}{x} = (-\frac{3}{10})^2$

b. $(-1.2 + x) \times 3 = (-3)^2 + 3$

⑥④ Consider integers a and b where $a > 0$ and $b < 0$. Justify your reasoning on whether each case yields a positive or a negative answer.

a. $(b - a)^2$

b. $b(a - b)$

Chapter 2

Exponents

2.1 Exponential Notation

Key Ideas

Exponential notation is a way to express repeated multiplication. Power, base, and exponent are components that are associated with exponential notation.

power – a number expression that represents repeated multiplication; it consists of a base and an exponent

base – the number in a power that is multiplied repeatedly

exponent – the number of times the base multiplies itself

$$\underset{\text{base}}{\overset{\text{power}\quad\text{exponent}}{5^3}} = 5 \times 5 \times 5$$

(5 is multiplied 3 times)

Examples

$3^2 \leftarrow$ Say "3 squared"; an exponent of 2 is called a square.

$= 3 \times 3$

$2^3 \leftarrow$ Say "2 cubed"; an exponent of 3 is called a cube.

$= 2 \times 2 \times 2$

$2^0 \leftarrow$ Any number raised to the power of 0 is 1.

$= 1$

$0^3 \leftarrow$ 0 raised to the power of any number is 0.

$= 0$

Try these!

Fill in the blanks.

① $2^2 = 2 \times \boxed{}$

② $3^3 = 3 \times 3 \times \boxed{}$

③ $4^3 = \boxed{} \times 4 \times 4$

④ $5^2 = 5 \times \boxed{}$

⑤ $\boxed{}^2 = 6 \times 6$

⑥ $\boxed{}^3 = 8 \times 8 \times 8$

⑦ $\boxed{}^4 = 3 \times 3 \times 3 \times 3$

⑧ $\boxed{}^3 = 7 \times 7 \times 7$

⑨ $10^{\boxed{}} = 1$

⑩ $4^{\boxed{}} = 4 \times 4 \times 4 \times 4$

⑪ $\boxed{}^8 = 0$

⑫ $9^{\boxed{}} = 9$

⑬ $3^{\boxed{}} = 3 \times 3 \times 3 \times 3 \times 3$

⑭ $5^{\boxed{}} = 5 \times 5 \times 5 \times 5 \times 5 \times 5 \times 5$

⑮ $7^{\boxed{}} = 7 \times 7 \times 7 \times 7 \times 7$

⑯ $\boxed{}^6 = 6 \times 6 \times 6 \times 6 \times 6 \times 6$

⑰ $\boxed{}^{\boxed{}} = 2 \times 2 \times 2 \times 2 \times 2$

⑱ $\boxed{}^{\boxed{}} = 8 \times 8 \times 8 \times 8 \times 8 \times 8 \times 8 \times 8$

Practice

Write each repeated multiplication as a power.

⑲ 2 x 2 x 2 x 2 = ______

⑳ 4 x 4 x 4 = ______

㉑ 5 x 5 x 5 = ______

㉒ 8 x 8 x 8 x 8 = ______

㉓ 7 x 7 x 7 x 7 x 7 = ______

㉔ 6 x 6 x 6 x 6 x 6 x 6 = ______

㉕ 12 = ______

㉖ 3 x 3 x 3 x 3 x 3 x 3 x 3 = ______

㉗ 0 x 0 x 0 x 0 = ______

㉘ 9 x 9 x 9 x 9 x 9 = ______

Write each power as a repeated multiplication.

㉙ 4^2 = ______

㉚ 5^3 = ______

㉛ 2^4 = ______

㉜ 3^5 = ______

㉝ 6^3 = ______

㉞ 8^4 = ______

㉟ 5^5 = ______

㊱ 0^6 = ______

㊲ 10^3 = ______

㊳ 7^1 = ______

Evaluate each power.

㊴ 3^2 = ______

㊵ 5^2 = ______

㊶ 7^2 = ______

㊷ 1^6 = ______

㊸ 3^4 = ______

㊹ 8^0 = ______

㊺ 4^3 = ______

㊻ 2^4 = ______

㊼ 0^{10} = ______

Express each as a product of powers.

㊽ 3 x 3 x 3 x 4 x 4 = ______

㊾ 5 x 2 x 5 x 2 x 2 = ______

㊿ 2 x 3 x 3 x 3 x 3 x 2 x 2 = ______

(51) 4 x 4 x 7 x 4 x 7 x 7 = ______

(52) 3 x 6 x 6 x 3 x 2 x 2 = ______

(53) 9 x 5 x 4 x 9 x 5 x 5 = ______

(54) 8 x 6 x 8 x 8 x 6 x 5 = ______

Hint

Group the same multipliers first. Then write them as powers.

e.g. 4 x 4 x 7 x 4 x 7 (base of 4; base of 7)

$= 4^3 \times 7^2$

Evaluate.

⑤⑤ $(-2)^2$

= (-2) × _____

= _____

⑤⑦ $(-4)^2$

= _____

= _____

⑤⑥ $(-3)^3$

= _____

= _____

⑤⑧ $(-5)^3$

= _____

= _____

Hint

Remember to include the negative sign in the base when evaluating each power.

e.g. $(-2)^3$

= (-2) × (-2) × (-2)

= -8

Compare the powers. Write ">" or "<".

⑤⑨ $2^4 \bigcirc 2^2$

⑥① $5^3 \bigcirc 5^4$

⑥③ $3^3 \bigcirc 1^3$

⑥⑤ $2^7 \bigcirc 3^7$

⑥⑦ $(-4)^3 \bigcirc (-2)^3$ ← Note: powers with negative bases

⑥⑨ $(-3)^3 \bigcirc 2^3$

⑥⓪ $3^2 \bigcirc 3^5$

⑥② $4^5 \bigcirc 4^3$

⑥④ $2^5 \bigcirc 4^5$

⑥⑥ $6^5 \bigcirc 5^5$

⑥⑧ $(-3)^2 \bigcirc (-3)^3$

⑦⓪ $5^4 \bigcirc (-3)^4$

Hint

Given that the bases of the powers are positive, consider the conditions below.

If the powers have the same base, then the one with the greater exponent is greater.

e.g. $3^2 < 3^4$ ← greater

If the powers have the same exponent, then the one with the greater base is greater.

e.g. $3^2 < 4^2$ ← greater

Write each number as a product of powers using the factor trees.

⑦①

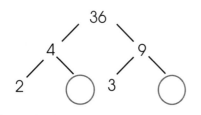

36 = 2 × _____ × 3 × _____

= _____ × _____

⑦②

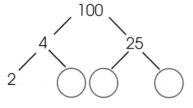

100 = _____

= _____

⑦③

16 = _____

= _____

⑦④

54 = _____

= _____

Answer the questions.

⑦⑤ Evaluate each power.

a. $(-3)^2$ b. $(-4)^2$ c. 3^3

d. -5^2 e. 10^3 f. -7^2

g. $(-8)^3$ h. 9^2 i. 20^0

j. $(-2)^4$ k. $(-5)^3$ l. -4^3

m. 0^5 n. $(-3)^0$ o. 5^3

p. $\left(\frac{2}{3}\right)^2$ q. $\left(\frac{1}{4}\right)^2$ r. $\left(\frac{1}{5}\right)^3$

s. $\left(-\frac{1}{3}\right)^3$ t. $\left(-\frac{2}{5}\right)^2$ u. $-\left(\frac{5}{7}\right)^2$

v. $-\left(\frac{2}{9}\right)^2$ w. $\left(-\frac{8}{11}\right)^0$ x. $-\left(\frac{3}{4}\right)^3$

> **Hint**
>
> Be careful with whether the negative sign in a negative number is part of the power.
>
> e.g. $-2^2 \neq (-2)^2$
>
> $-(2 \times 2) = -4$ $(-2) \times (-2) = 4$
>
> Powers with fractions as bases are also evaluated through multiplication.
>
> e.g. $\left(\frac{1}{2}\right)^2 = \frac{1}{2} \times \frac{1}{2} = \frac{1}{4}$

⑦⑥ Express each integer as two different powers.

a. 9   b. 25   c. 49   d. 16   e. -1

f. 81   g. 0   h. 625   i. -4   j. -64

⑦⑦ Kyle thinks that all perfect squares can be expressed as two different powers each with an exponent of 2. Is he correct? Explain.

⑦⑧ Express each number as a product of powers with prime numbers as bases.

a. 250   b. 144   c. 324   d. 600   e. 1350

⑦⑨ Explain the difference between $(-2)^4$ and -2^4.

⑧⓪ Consider a^b where $a < 0$.

a. Write a condition of b when $a^b > 0$.

b. Write a condition of b when $a^b < 0$.

⑧① The number of weed plants in a controlled environment doubles every 3 months. If there were 10 weed plants in the beginning, how many will there be in 2 years?

Chapter 2

2.2 Laws of Exponents

Key Ideas

Laws of exponents are important because they offer us a quick way to perform operations to simplify expressions.

Laws of Exponents

For $a \neq 0$, p is an integer and m and n are natural numbers.

Product of Powers	$a^m \times a^n = a^{m+n}$	← same base
Quotient of Powers	$a^m \div a^n = a^{m-n}$	← same base
Power of a Power	$(a^m)^n = a^{mn}$	
Negative Exponent	$a^{-p} = \dfrac{1}{a^p}$	
Identity Exponent	$a^1 = a$	
Zero Exponent	$a^0 = 1$	

Examples

$4^3 \times 4^2$

$= 4 \times 4 \times 4 \times 4 \times 4$

$= \underline{4^5}$

$4^3 \times 4^2$ ← product of powers

$= 4^{3+2}$ ← adding the exponents

$= \underline{4^5}$

$4^5 \div 4^2$

$= \dfrac{4 \times 4 \times 4 \times \cancel{4}^1 \times \cancel{4}^1}{\cancel{4}_1 \times \cancel{4}_1}$

$= \underline{4^3}$

$4^5 \div 4^2$ ← quotient of powers

$= 4^{5-2}$ ← subtracting the exponents

$= \underline{4^3}$

$(4^3)^2$

$= 4^3 \times 4^3$

$= 4 \times 4 \times 4 \times 4 \times 4 \times 4$

$= \underline{4^6}$

$(4^3)^2$ ← power of a power

$= 4^{3 \times 2}$ ← multiplying the exponents

$= \underline{4^6}$

Try these!

Fill in the blanks.

① $a^m \times a^n = a^{m+n}$

a. $5^3 \times 5^2 = 5^{\boxed{} + \boxed{}}$

      $= 5^{\boxed{}}$

b. $7^2 \times 7^4 = \boxed{}^{2+4}$

      $= \boxed{}^{6}$

② $a^m \div a^n = a^{m-n}$

a. $5^3 \div 5^2 = 5^{\boxed{} - \boxed{}}$

      $= 5^{\boxed{}}$

b. $2^6 \div 2^2 = \boxed{}^{6-2}$

      $= \boxed{}^{4}$

③ $(a^m)^n = a^{mn}$

a. $(2^3)^5 = 2^{\boxed{} \times \boxed{}}$

      $= 2^{\boxed{}}$

b. $(3^4)^2 = \boxed{}^{4 \times 2}$

      $= \boxed{}^{8}$

④ $a^{-p} = \dfrac{1}{a^p}$

a. $5^{-2} = \dfrac{1}{5^{\boxed{}}}$

b. $3^{-6} = \dfrac{1}{\boxed{}^{6}}$

⑤ $a^1 = a$

a. $7^1 = \boxed{}$

b. $6^1 = \boxed{}$

⑥ $a^0 = 1$

a. $5^0 = \boxed{}$

b. $4^0 = \boxed{}$

Fill in the blanks.

⑦ a. $3^2 \times 3^5 = 3^{\quad+} = $ _____

b. $4^8 \div 4^6 = 4^{\quad-} = $ _____

c. $(6^3)^4 = 6^{\quad\times} = $ _____

d. $(4^2)^5 = 4^{\quad\times} = $ _____

e. $3^{-2} = \dfrac{1}{3}$

f. $4^0 = $ _____

g. $5^1 = $ _____

h. $2^{-5} = $ _____

i. $9^0 = $ _____

j. $2^0 = $ _____

k. $4^{-3} = $ _____

l. $3^{-4} = $ _____

Evaluate each multiplication or division of powers. Write the answer as a single power. Show your work.

⑧ $3^2 \times 3^4$

⑨ $5^3 \times 5^2$

⑩ $6^4 \times 6^2$

⑪ $8^4 \div 8^3$

= _____

= _____

⑫ $10^5 \div 10^3$

⑬ $10^5 \div 10^1$

⑭ $2^0 \times 2^7$

⑮ $7^9 \div 7^0$

Write each answer as a single power.

⑯ $(2^3)^2 = $ _____

⑰ $(4^2)^3 = $ _____

⑱ $(8^5)^2 = $ _____

⑲ $(10^2)^2 = $ _____

⑳ $(3^2)^4 = $ _____

㉑ $(8^0)^7 = $ _____

㉒ $(9^2)^5 = $ _____

㉓ $(4^6)^5 = $ _____

Express each answer as a power with a positive exponent.

㉔ 2^{-2}

㉕ 5^{-2}

㉖ 10^{-3}

㉗ 6^{-2}

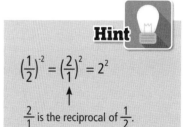

Hint

$$\left(\frac{1}{2}\right)^{-2} = \left(\frac{2}{1}\right)^{2} = 2^2$$

$\frac{2}{1}$ is the reciprocal of $\frac{1}{2}$.

㉘ 3^{-3}

㉙ $\left(\dfrac{1}{3}\right)^{-2}$

㉚ $\left(\dfrac{1}{5}\right)^{-3}$

㉛ $\left(\dfrac{2}{3}\right)^{-2}$

Simplify each expression and write the answer as a power. Show your work.

㉜ $4^2 \times 4^6 \times 4^{-3}$

㉝ $8^3 \times 8^{-6} \times 8^2$

㉞ $7^6 \div 7^3 \div 7^2$

㉟ $8^6 \div 8^{-5} \div 8^{-2}$

㊱ $9^3 \times 9^2 \div 9^4$

㊲ $5^8 \div 5^5 \times 5^{-6}$

㊳ $4^0 \times 4^6 \div 4^{-1}$

㊴ $5^6 \times 5^1 \div 5^{-3}$

㊵ $7^6 \div 7^{-1} \div 7^0$

㊶ $6^4 \times 6^{-2} \times 6^{-3}$

㊷ $4^3 \div 4^2 \div 4^5$

㊸ $3^5 \times 3^{-2} \div 3^7$

Simplify each expression. Write the answer as a product of powers.

㊹ $4^2 \times 3^2 \times 4^3 \div 3^3$

㊺ $5^6 \times 3^3 \div 5^2 \times 3^4$

Hint

Group the powers with the same base before simplifying.

e.g. $\quad 2^4 \times 3^2 \div 2^2 \times 3^4$
$= 2^4 \div 2^2 \times 3^2 \times 3^4$
$= 2^2 \times 3^6$

㊻ $4^{-2} \times 6^3 \times 6^2 \div 4^3$

㊼ $3^2 \times 7^4 \times 3^0 \times 7^{-1}$

㊽ $5^4 \times 2^{-5} \div 2^{-3} \times 5 \div 5^5$

㊾ $9^{-3} \times 8^{-4} \div 9^2 \times 9^0 \times 8^{-5} \div 9^2$

Hint: $\div 9^{-2} \rightarrow \times 9^2 \qquad \div 7^6 \rightarrow \times 7^{-6}$

㊿ $2^5 \times 7^2 \div 2^6 \times 3^{-3} \times 7^{-2} \times 3$

(51) $10^4 \div 9^{-2} \times 10^{-2} \div 7^6 \times 9^3 \div 7^2$

Simplify each expression and write the answer as a power.

(52) a. $2^3 \times 2^0$ b. $4^{-2} \times 4^3$
c. $9^2 \div 9^{-1} \times 9^2$ d. $3^7 \div 3^{-1} \div 3^{-2}$
e. $10^3 \times 10^{-1} \div 10^2$ f. $8^5 \div 8^3 \div 8^{-1}$
g. $(-5)^3 \times (-5)^4 \div (-5)^2$ h. $(-2)^{-2} \times (-2)^{-3} \div (-2)^4$
i. $(-6)^4 \times (-6) \times (-6)^{-3}$ j. $(-7)^3 \div (-7)^2 \times (-7)^{-5}$

(53) a. $(3^{-2})^2 \times (3^4)^{-1}$ b. $(5^2)^{-2} \div (5^{-1})^3$
c. $(4^7)^1 \times (4^{-2})^{-2}$ d. $(8^2)^{-1} \div (8^{-1})^2$
e. $((-6)^{-1})^2 \times ((-6)^3)^{-1}$ f. $((-3)^4)^{-2} \times ((-3)^1)^{-1}$
g. $((-2)^3)^{-2} \div (2^{-3})^{-1}$ h. $(4^2)^2 \div ((-4)^{-1})^{-2}$

(54) a. $9^2 \times 3^4$ b. $2^2 \times 4^2$
c. $4 \times 2^3 \div 8^{-1}$ d. $3^0 \times 9^{-2} \times 81$
e. $1 \times 9^2 \times 3^{-2}$ f. $25 \times 5^{-4} \times 125$
g. $\frac{1}{16} \times 2^{-5} \div 4^{-3}$ h. $\frac{1}{9} \times 3^{-3} \times (9^{-2})^{-1}$
i. $8^{-2} \times \frac{1}{4} \times 2^8$ j. $\frac{1}{7^{-2}} \div 343 \times (7^{-1})^2$
k. $16^2 \times 2^{-5} \div (\frac{1}{4})^3$ l. $(\frac{9}{4})^2 \div (\frac{2}{3})^{-2} \times \frac{8}{27}$

Note

Laws of Exponents

$a \neq 0$, p – integer,
m and n – natural numbers

$a^m \times a^n = a^{m+n}$
$a^m \div a^n = a^{m-n}$
$(a^m)^n = a^{mn}$
$a^{-p} = \frac{1}{a^p}$
$a^1 = a$
$a^0 = 1$

Hint

Rewrite powers so that all powers in an expression have the same base.

e.g. $4 \times 2^4 \div 8^2$
$= 2^2 \times 2^4 \div (2^3)^2$ ← All bases are 2.
$= 2^2 \times 2^4 \div 2^6$
$= 2^0$
$= 1$

Answer the questions.

(55) A container is 8 inches tall. How many $\frac{1}{32}$-inch-thick coins can be stacked and still fit in the container?

(56) Describe the steps to evaluate $(-2)^{-3}$.

(57) Can $\frac{1}{64}$ be expressed as a single power in more than one way? If so, list three ways with negative exponents and three ways with positive exponents.

(58) A Mersenne prime is a prime number that is one less than a power of two. $M = 2^n - 1$. So, $2^2 - 1 = 3$ is a Mersenne prime, while $2^4 - 1 = 15$ is not because 15 is not a prime number. Find the next two Mersenne primes that come after 3.

(59) Consider $(a^x)^y$ where $a > 0$, $x \neq 0$, and $y \neq 0$. Determine the conditions of x and y when $(a^x)^y > 0$.

(60) Abby thinks that all integers can be expressed as more than one power. Is she correct? Explain.

Chapter 2

2.3 Operations with Powers

Key Ideas

In the order of operations, evaluating numbers with exponents comes right after evaluating operations within brackets. For efficiency, try to simplify powers before converting them into large numbers. Often times, quotient of powers and product of powers can be simplified. Being familiar with the rules below is helpful when simplifying.

$$(ab)^m = a^m b^m$$

$$\left(\frac{a}{b}\right)^m = \frac{a^m}{b^m}, \, b \neq 0$$

Examples

$$\frac{(4 \times 5)^2}{5^2}$$
$$= \frac{20^2}{5^2}$$
$$= \frac{400}{25}$$
$$= 16$$

$$\frac{(4 \times 5)^2}{5^2}$$
$$= \frac{4^2 \times \cancel{5^2}}{\cancel{5^2}}$$
$$= 4^2$$
$$= 16 \quad \checkmark \text{more efficient}$$

$$\frac{6^3}{3^3}$$
$$= \frac{216}{27}$$
$$= 8$$

$$\frac{6^3}{3^3}$$
$$= \left(\frac{6}{3}\right)^3$$
$$= 2^3$$
$$= 8 \quad \checkmark \text{more efficient}$$

Simplify each expression into a single power.

Try these!

① a. $(2 \times 7)^6 = 2^6 \times 7^{\boxed{}}$

b. $(4 \times 5)^4 = 4^{\boxed{}} \times 5^4$

c. $(3 \times 2)^5 = 3^{\boxed{}} \times 2^{\boxed{}}$

d. $5^8 \times 3^8 = (5 \times 3)^{\boxed{}}$

e. $4^9 \times 6^9 = (4 \times \boxed{})^9$

f. $5^3 \times 2^3 = (\boxed{} \times 2)^{\boxed{}}$

② a. $\left(\frac{3}{10}\right)^4 = \frac{3^{\boxed{}}}{10^4}$

b. $\left(\frac{1}{4}\right)^6 = \frac{1^6}{4^{\boxed{}}}$

c. $\left(\frac{5}{8}\right)^2 = \frac{5^{\boxed{}}}{8^{\boxed{}}}$

d. $\frac{3^5}{7^5} = \left(\frac{3}{7}\right)^{\boxed{}}$

e. $\frac{2^3}{9^3} = \left(\frac{\boxed{}}{9}\right)^3$

f. $\frac{6^4}{7^4} = \left(\frac{6}{\boxed{}}\right)^{\boxed{}}$

③ a. $\frac{8^6 \times 8^2}{8^3} = 8^{\boxed{}}$

b. $\frac{11^7}{11^2 \times 11^3} = 11^{\boxed{}}$

c. $\frac{4^3 \times 4^5}{4^2 \times 4^3} = 4^{\boxed{}}$

d. $\frac{(-2)^3 \times (-2)}{(-2)^2} = (-2)^{\boxed{}}$

e. $\frac{(-3)^3}{(-3) \times (-3)} = (-3)^{\boxed{}}$

f. $\frac{(-5)^2 \times (-5)}{(-5) \times (-5)^3} = (-5)^{\boxed{}}$

④ a. $(3^2)^4 \times 3^2 = 3^{\boxed{}}$

b. $(4^3)^2 \times 4 = 4^{\boxed{}}$

c. $(8^2)^2 \times (8^2)^2 = 8^{\boxed{}}$

d. $(5^4)^2 \div 5^3 = 5^{\boxed{}}$

e. $(7^3)^3 \div (7^2)^3 = 7^{\boxed{}}$

f. $((-9)^3)^2 \div (-9)^2 = (-9)^{\boxed{}}$

Fill in the missing numbers.

⑤ $4^{\square} \div 4^4 = 4^3$

⑥ $2^5 \times 2^{\square} = 2^8$

⑦ $3^4 \times \square^2 = 3^6$

⑧ $\dfrac{4^{\square}}{4^5} = 4^{-2}$

⑨ $\dfrac{2^8}{2^{\square}} = 2^5$

⑩ $\dfrac{3^{\square}}{3^{11}} = 3^{-5}$

⑪ $3^2 \times 3^{\square} \div 3^3 = 3^4$

⑫ $\left(\dfrac{10}{3}\right)^2 = \dfrac{10^{\square}}{3^{\square}}$

⑬ $\left(\dfrac{9}{7}\right)^{\square} = \dfrac{9^{\square}}{7^{-2}}$

⑭ $(2^2)^{\square} = 2^8$

⑮ $(5^{\square})^3 = 5^{15}$

⑯ $\dfrac{(-8)^{\square}}{(-8)^6} = 8^{-2}$

Simplify each expression into a power or rewrite as a product of powers.

⑰   a. $\dfrac{7^5 \times 7^2}{7^3} =$ _____

b. $\dfrac{10^3}{10 \times 10^{-4}} =$ _____

c. $\dfrac{6^7 \times 6^2}{6^5 \times 6^{-2}} =$ _____

d. $(5^2)^2 \times 5 =$ _____

e. $(6^4)^2 \times (6^2)^{-3} =$ _____

f. $((-8)^3)^3 \div (-8)^5 =$ _____

⑱   a. $(3 \times 4)^5 = 3^5 \times$ _____

b. $(7 \times 9)^2 =$ _____

c. $(6 \times 8)^{-3} =$ _____

d. $2^6 \times 3^6 = (2 \times \text{_____})^6$

e. $5^3 \times 4^3 =$ _____

f. $-3^{-10} \times 2^{-10} =$ _____

⑲   a. $\left(\dfrac{5}{6}\right)^2 = \dfrac{(\quad)^2}{(\quad)^2}$

b. $\left(\dfrac{2}{7}\right)^3 =$ _____

c. $\left(\dfrac{3}{8}\right)^{-4} =$ _____

d. $\dfrac{7^4}{3^4} = \left(\dfrac{\quad}{\quad}\right)^4$

e. $\dfrac{8^3}{9^3} =$ _____

f. $\dfrac{(-4)^{-5}}{9^{-5}} =$ _____

Evaluate the powers.

⑳   a. $3^3 =$ _____

b. $(-2)^3 =$ _____

c. $(-3)^4 =$ _____

d. $(-5)^2 =$ _____

e. $3^{-2} =$ _____

f. $6^{-3} =$ _____

㉑   a. $\left(\dfrac{1}{3}\right)^2 =$ _____

b. $\left(\dfrac{2}{3}\right)^2 =$ _____

c. $\left(\dfrac{4}{5}\right)^{-1} =$ _____

d. $\left(\dfrac{2}{5}\right)^{-2} =$ _____

e. $\left(\dfrac{3}{2}\right)^{-3} =$ _____

f. $\left(\dfrac{4}{3}\right)^{-2} =$ _____

㉒   a. $0.1^2 =$ _____

b. $0.5^2 =$ _____

c. $0.2^{-3} =$ _____

d. $(-0.2)^3 =$ _____

e. $(-0.3)^3 =$ _____

f. $(-0.4)^2 =$ _____

Express each power with the given base. Show your work.

㉓ with a base of 2

    a. 4^2 b. 16^2 c. 8^3

       $= (2^{})^2$

       $= 2^{}$

Hint

Rewrite each power with the given base. Then simplify.

e.g. Express 8^4 with a base of 2.

$$8^4$$
$$= (2^3)^4 \leftarrow 8 = 2^3$$
$$= 2^{12}$$

㉔ with a base of 3

    a. 9^3 b. 27^2 c. $(9^2)^3$

㉕ with a base of 5

    a. 25^3 b. $(125^2)^2$

㉖ with a base of -4

    a. 16^2 b. -64^3

Simplify each expression into a power and evaluate. Show your work.

㉗ $\dfrac{(3^2)(3^2)}{3^3}$

㉘ $\dfrac{(4^2)(4^3)}{4^6}$

㉙ $\dfrac{(5^{-3})(5^4)}{5^2}$

㉚ $\dfrac{6^3}{(6^{-2})(6^4)}$

㉛ $\dfrac{(3^{-3})(3^2)}{(3^2)(3^{-1})}$

㉜ $\dfrac{(2^5)(2^4)}{(2^8)(2^{-2})}$

㉝ $\dfrac{(4^2)^2}{(4^3)(4^2)}$

㉞ $\dfrac{((-2)^2)^3(-2)^2}{(-2)^4}$

㉟ $\left(\dfrac{(5^2)^3}{5^4}\right)^2$

㊱ $\left(\dfrac{6^4}{(6^{-1})(6^4)}\right)^3$

㊲ $\left(\dfrac{(9^{-2})(9^3)}{9^2}\right)^{-1}$

㊳ $\dfrac{(7^4)^{-2}}{(7^{-3})(7^{-4})}$

㊴ $\dfrac{4^2}{(2^4)(2^2)}$

㊵ $\dfrac{(9^2)(3^2)}{3^4}$

㊶ $\dfrac{(25^2)^3}{(5^3)(5^5)}$

Simplify each expression into a product of powers. Show your work.

㊷ $\dfrac{(2^3)(3^4)(2^{-2})}{(3^{-5})(3^6)}$

㊸ $\dfrac{(-4)^2\,(3^{-2})}{(-3)^2(3^3)(4^5)}$

㊹ $\dfrac{(2\times3)^3}{2^{-6}\times3^{-2}}$

㊺ $(3^2\times2^5)^2\,(3^3\times2^4)^3$

㊻ $(4^2\times5^3)^{-2}\,(4^3\times5^2)^2$

㊼ $\dfrac{((-4)^2\times5)^2}{(-4\times5)^{-4}}$

㊽ $\dfrac{(7^2\times3^2)^3}{(3^{-2})(7^{-5})^2}$

㊾ $\dfrac{(9^3\times2^5)^3}{(2^5\times(-9)^2)^4}$

㊿ $\dfrac{((-3)^3\times5^2)^3}{(5^{-4}\times(-3)^{-3})^{-2}}$

Convert the numbers in the binary system into the decimal system. Show your work.

(51) 110 ➔ $1 \times 2^2 + 1 \times 2^1 + 0 \times 2^0$

= ______ + ______ + ______

= ______

(52) 1010 ➔ 1×2^3 + ____________________

= ______ + ______ + ______ + ______

= ______

(53) 1001 ➔ ____________________

= ____________________

= ____________________

Hint

Binary numbers are base-2 numbers with two values – 0 and 1.

Numbers in the Decimal System

e.g. 103 ➔ $1 \times 10^2 + 0 \times 10^1 + 3 \times 10^0$

$= 100 + 0 + 3$

$= 103$

Numbers in the Binary System

e.g. 101 ➔ $1 \times 2^2 + 0 \times 2^1 + 1 \times 2^0$

$= 4 + 0 + 1$

$= 5$

101 in the binary system means 5 in the decimal system.

(54) 11010

(55) 10111

(56) 10001

(57) 110110

For each statement, write "T" for true and "F" for false.

(58) The numbers that represent the values 0 and 1 are the same in the binary system and the decimal system. ______

(59) The largest value for a 7-digit binary number is 127. ______

(60) Consider two binary numbers that have the same number of digits. The one that has more 1s has a greater value. ______

Answer the questions.

㊱ Explain why 2^8 can be expressed as a power with a base of 4, but 2^7 cannot.

Note

$$(ab)^m = a^m b^m$$
$$\left(\frac{a}{b}\right)^m = \frac{a^m}{b^m}, b \neq 0$$

㊲ Describe the steps needed to convert a power into another power with a smaller base. Use 81^3 as an example.

㊳ For each power below, list the possible positive bases it can be converted into as a single power.

a. 64   b. 100   c. 729

㊴ Rewrite each power with the given base.

a. $(27^3)^2 = 3$ b. $(-8)^2 = (-2)$ c. $((-25)^2)^3 = 5$

㊵ Explain why a power with a base of 0 cannot have a negative exponent.

㊶ Look at Tim's solution below. Is it correct? If not, make the correction.

$$(4.5^3)(1.5)^{-2}$$
$$= \frac{4.5^3}{1.5^2}$$
$$= \left(\frac{4.5}{1.5}\right)^3$$
$$= 3^3$$

㊷ Consider a cube that has a volume of $(2^5)^3$ cm^3. Without evaluating, find and write its side length as a power and its surface area as a product of powers.

㊸ A binary counter contains 6 digits. What is the highest decimal number that it can count to?

Hint

㊹ Consider these binary numbers: 111, 10101, and 100100.

a. Find their sum and write it as a power of 2.

b. Write the answer in Question 69a as a binary number.

Convert the binary numbers into decimal numbers and add to find the sum.

M A T H   I R L

Have you heard of the number called "googol"? It is numerically 10^{1000} which is 1 followed by one hundred zeros! And when you think it is already a large number, there are even larger numbers – googolplex! It is 10^{googol} or $10^{10^{1000}}$ numerically. Scan the QR code to learn more about large numbers.

Chapter 2

2.4 Squares and Square Roots

Key Ideas

Squares are powers with an exponent of 2. When a number is raised to the power of 2, we say the number is squared. On the other hand, square roots are the opposite of squares.

Square Root Rules

Consider $a \geq 0$.

- $\sqrt{a} \times \sqrt{a} = a$
- $\sqrt{a^2} = a$

Consider $a, b \geq 0$.

- $\sqrt{ab} = \sqrt{a} \times \sqrt{b}$
- $\sqrt{\dfrac{a}{b}} = \dfrac{\sqrt{a}}{\sqrt{b}}$, where $b \neq 0$
- If $a^2 = b$, then $\sqrt{b} = a$.

Examples

$$\sqrt{9} \times \sqrt{9} = 9 \quad \longleftarrow \sqrt{a} \times \sqrt{a} = a$$
$$\uparrow \qquad \uparrow$$
$$3 \qquad 3$$

$$\sqrt{9^2} = 9 \quad \longleftarrow \sqrt{a^2} = a$$
$$\uparrow$$
$$\sqrt{81}$$

$$\sqrt{36} = \sqrt{4} \times \sqrt{9} \quad \longleftarrow \sqrt{ab} = \sqrt{a} \times \sqrt{b}$$
$$\uparrow \qquad \uparrow \qquad \uparrow$$
$$6 \qquad 2 \qquad 3$$

$$\sqrt{\dfrac{9}{4}} = \dfrac{\sqrt{9}}{\sqrt{4}} \quad \longleftarrow \sqrt{\dfrac{a}{b}} = \dfrac{\sqrt{a}}{\sqrt{b}}$$
$$\uparrow \qquad \uparrow$$
$$\dfrac{3}{2} \qquad \dfrac{3}{2}$$

$$4^2 = 16, \text{ so } \sqrt{16} = 4 \quad \longleftarrow \begin{array}{l} a^2 = b \\ \sqrt{b} = a \end{array}$$

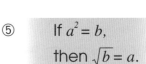

Try these!

Fill in the blanks.

① $\sqrt{a} \times \sqrt{a} = a$

   a. $\sqrt{4} \times \sqrt{4} = \boxed{}$

   b. $\sqrt{10} \times \sqrt{10} = \boxed{}$

② $\sqrt{a^2} = a$

   a. $\sqrt{16^2} = \boxed{}$

   b. $\sqrt{20^2} = \boxed{}$

③ $\sqrt{ab} = \sqrt{a} \times \sqrt{b}$

   a. $\sqrt{9 \times 16} = \sqrt{9} \times \sqrt{\boxed{}}$

   b. $\sqrt{25 \times 2} = \sqrt{25} \times \sqrt{\boxed{}}$

④ $\sqrt{\dfrac{a}{b}} = \dfrac{\sqrt{a}}{\sqrt{b}}$

   a. $\sqrt{\dfrac{100}{4}} = \dfrac{\sqrt{100}}{\sqrt{\boxed{}}}$

   b. $\sqrt{\dfrac{16}{4}} = \dfrac{\sqrt{\boxed{}}}{\sqrt{4}}$

⑤ If $a^2 = b$, then $\sqrt{b} = a$.

   a. $\quad 5^2 = 25$

      $\sqrt{25} = \boxed{}$

   b. $\quad 4.5^2 = 20.25$

      $\sqrt{20.25} = \boxed{}$

   c. $\left(\dfrac{3}{4}\right)^2 = \dfrac{9}{16}$

      $\sqrt{\dfrac{9}{16}} = \boxed{}$

Evaluate each square root without using a calculator.

⑥ $\sqrt{5^2}$ = _____

⑦ $\sqrt{8} \times \sqrt{8}$ = _____

⑧ $\sqrt{10^2}$ = _____

⑨ $\sqrt{7} \times \sqrt{7}$ = _____

⑩ $\sqrt{12^2}$ = _____

⑪ $(\sqrt{3.5})^2$ = _____

⑫ $\sqrt{4 \times 4}$ = _____

⑬ $\sqrt{2} \times \sqrt{32}$ = _____

⑭ $\sqrt{4.5 \times 2}$ = _____

⑮ $\sqrt{\dfrac{36}{9}}$ = _____

⑯ $\sqrt{\dfrac{8}{0.5}}$ = _____

⑰ $\dfrac{\sqrt{18}}{\sqrt{2}}$ = _____

Simplify the square roots. Show your work.

⑱ $\sqrt{12}$

$= \sqrt{ \times 3}$

$= \sqrt{} \times \sqrt{3}$

$= \sqrt{3}$

⑲ $\sqrt{20}$

Hint

To simplify a square root, first rewrite the number within the root as a product of the largest perfect square possible and another number. Then find the square roots to simplify.

e.g. $\sqrt{75}$

$= \sqrt{25 \times 3}$ ← 25 is the largest perfect square possible.

$= \sqrt{25} \times \sqrt{3}$

$= 5\sqrt{3}$

⑳ $\sqrt{27}$

㉑ $\sqrt{50}$

㉒ $\sqrt{32}$

㉓ $\sqrt{54}$

㉔ $\sqrt{48}$

㉕ $\sqrt{72}$ = _____

㉖ $\sqrt{120}$ = _____

㉗ $\sqrt{150}$ = _____

㉘ $\sqrt{200}$ = _____

㉙ $\sqrt{243}$ = _____

㉚ $\sqrt{363}$ = _____

Evaluate and write your answers in simplest form. Show your work.

③① $\sqrt{12} \times \sqrt{8}$

③② $\sqrt{32} \times \sqrt{18}$

③③ $2\sqrt{5} \times \sqrt{10}$

③④ $3\sqrt{6} \times 2\sqrt{24}$

③⑤ $\sqrt{80} \div \sqrt{10}$

③⑥ $3\sqrt{6} \div \sqrt{18}$

③⑦ $\sqrt{\dfrac{3}{4}} \times \sqrt{\dfrac{2}{9}}$

③⑧ $\sqrt{\dfrac{4}{5}} \times \sqrt{20}$

③⑨ $\sqrt{150} \div 3\sqrt{5}$

④⓪ $5\sqrt{2} \div 2\sqrt{5}$

④① $\dfrac{2\sqrt{8} \times 3\sqrt{2}}{2}$

④② $\dfrac{5\sqrt{5}}{\sqrt{125} \times \sqrt{2}}$

④③ $\dfrac{\sqrt{8} \times 4\sqrt{3}}{8\sqrt{15}}$

Answer the questions.

㊹ Evaluate the expressions.

a. $\sqrt{6} + 2\sqrt{2} \times 3\sqrt{3}$

b. $(-(\sqrt{5^2}) + (-1)) \times (\sqrt{2})^2$

> **Hint**
>
> In the order of operations, square roots are ranked the same as exponents.

c. $(4\sqrt{8} \div 2\sqrt{2}) - (\sqrt{2} \times \sqrt{8})^2$

d. $\dfrac{(\sqrt{32})(\sqrt{2})^{-1}}{(-1+3)^2}$

> e.g. $(\sqrt{36} - 2^2) \times (-5)$
>
> $= (6 - 4) \times (-5)$
>
> $= -10$

e. $\dfrac{\sqrt{3^2} \times 5\sqrt{2}}{\sqrt{18}}$

f. $\dfrac{\sqrt{15} \times \sqrt{24}}{\sqrt{4+1}}$

㊺ Simon says, "$\sqrt{-2} \times \sqrt{-2} = -2$. So -2 has a square root." Is he correct? Explain.

㊻ Consider $a \geq 0$. Show that $\sqrt{a^2} = a$.

㊼ Prove each of the following inequality using a counter example.

a. $\sqrt{a+b} \neq \sqrt{a} + \sqrt{b}$

b. $\sqrt{a-b} \neq \sqrt{a} - \sqrt{b}$

c. $\sqrt{a^2 + b^2} \neq a + b$

㊽ Give an example to show that the square root of a negative number cannot be evaluated.

㊾ A square-based garden has an area of 50 m².

a. What is the side length of the garden?

b. What is the perimeter of the garden?

㊿ A rectangular container has the dimensions of $3\sqrt{2}$ m by $2\sqrt{5}$ m by $\sqrt{10}$ m.

a. What is its surface area?

b. What is its volume?

(51) A frame is in the shape of an isosceles right triangle. The identical sides have lengths of $5\sqrt{3}$ m each.

a. What is the length of the hypotenuse?

b. What is the perimeter?

Chapter 2

2.5 Scientific Notation

Key Ideas

Scientific notation is a way of writing very large or very small numbers. It is a product of a decimal and a power of 10. The magnitude* of the decimal must be from 1 to 10 (excluding 10) and the exponent of the power indicates how small or large the number is.

Numbers in Scientific Notation

$$a \times 10^{n} \leftarrow \text{an integer}$$

$1 \le$ magnitude of $a < 10$ power of 10

* The magnitude of a number is its distance from zero. For example, the magnitude of 5 is 5 and the magnitude of -2 is 2.

Examples

Write the numbers in scientific notation.

$5,8\,2\,9. = 5.829 \times 10^3$ $\leftarrow$ Moved the decimal point 3 places to the left.

$0.0\,2\,8\,9 = 2.89 \times 10^{-2}$ $\leftarrow$ Moved the decimal point 2 places to the right.

Write the numbers the scientific notation represents.

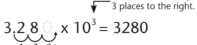

$3.2\,8\,0 \times 10^3 = 3280$

Move the decimal point 3 places to the left.

$0.0\,0\,3.2\,8 \times 10^{-3} = 0.00328$

Try these!

Fill in the blanks to write the numbers in scientific notation. Draw arrows to help you.

① **For Large Numbers**
- move decimal point to the left
- have powers of 10 with positive exponents

a. $2,3\,8\,9. = 2.389 \times 10^{\boxed{}}$

b. $4\,3\,2\,0\,0 = \boxed{} \times 10^4$

c. $9\,0\,2\,7\,1 = 9.0271 \times 10^{\boxed{}}$

d. $3\,6\,0\,0\,2\,8 = \boxed{} \times 10^5$

e. $5\,2\,0\,1\,0\,0 = 5.201 \times 10^{\boxed{}}$

f. $1\,0\,2\,0\,4\,7 = \boxed{} \times 10^5$

② **For Small Numbers**
- move decimal point to the right
- have powers of 10 with negative exponents

a. $0.9 = 9 \times 10^{\boxed{}}$

b. $0.7\,2\,3 = \boxed{} \times 10^{-1}$

c. $0.0\,8\,4 = 8.4 \times 10^{\boxed{}}$

d. $0.0\,0\,4\,9 = \boxed{} \times 10^{-3}$

e. $0.0\,0\,0\,9\,2\,4 = 9.24 \times 10^{\boxed{}}$

f. $0.0\,0\,0\,0\,5\,1 = \boxed{} \times 10^{-5}$

Write each number in scientific notation.

③ 5000   = _____

④ 0.04   = _____

⑤ 0.052   = _____

⑥ 24 080   = _____

⑦ 300 700   = _____

⑧ -0.0409   = _____

⑨ 0.008   = _____

⑩ 1 085 000 = _____

⑪ -0.000245 = _____

⑫ 7 903 100 = _____

Write the numbers in scientific notation in standard form.

⑬ a. 3×10^2 = _____

b. 2.2×10^3 = _____

c. 4.05×10^4 = _____

d. -5.12×10^5 = _____

⑭ a. 6×10^{-2} = _____

b. 9.1×10^{-3} = _____

c. 1.743×10^{-4} = _____

d. -8×10^{-5} = _____

> **Hint**
>
> $a \times 10^n$ ← shows how many places to move the decimal point
>
> If n is positive, move the decimal point to the right.
>
> e.g. $4.01 \times 10^3 = 4010$
>
> If n is negative, move the decimal point to the left.
>
> e.g. $4.01 \times 10^{-3} = 0.00401$

Check if each number is in scientific notation. If not, write it in scientific notation.

⑮ 25×10^{-2} = _____

⑯ 0.8×10^{-3} = _____

⑰ -2.5×10^3 = _____

⑱ 10×10^2 = _____

⑲ 0.66×10^4 = _____

⑳ 590×10^{-2} = _____

㉑ -1.7×10^{-3} = _____

㉒ -11×10^3 = _____

㉓ 0.1×10^{-1} = _____

㉔ 9000×10^{-4} = _____

Compare the numbers. Write "<", ">", or "=".

㉕ 3.4×10^2 ◯ 3.6×10^2

㉖ 8×10^{-2} ◯ 8×10^{-3}

㉗ 7.9×10^3 ◯ 2×10^4

㉘ 3.06×10^4 ◯ 3.6×10^3

㉙ 1.2×10^{-3} ◯ 4×10^{-2}

㉚ 1079 ◯ 1.079×10^3

㉛ 7.1×10^{-1} ◯ 710

㉜ 2.88×10^{-2} ◯ 2.8×10^2

㉝ 6.02×10^2 ◯ 6.2×10^{-3}

㉞ 5.01×10^{-3} ◯ 0.00501

Evaluate. Write the answers in scientific notation. Show your work.

㉟ $5 \times 10^3 \times 3$

$=$ _____ $\times 10^3$

$=$ _____ $\times 10^4$

㊱ $4 \times 10^2 \div 5$

> **Hint**
>
> When multiplying or dividing numbers in scientific notation, rearrange to group the decimals and the powers for easier calculation.
>
> e.g. $(2.4 \times 10^5) \div (5 \times 10^2)$
> $= (2.4 \div 5) \times (10^5 \div 10^2)$
> $= 0.48 \times 10^3$
> $= 4.8 \times 10^2$

㊲ $7 \times 10^{-2} \times 2$

㊳ $8 \times 10^{-1} \div 20$

㊳9 $(1.2 \times 10^3) \times (3 \times 10^2)$

㊵ $(-2.5 \times 10^2) \div (5 \times 10^1)$

㊶ $(3.6 \times 10^{-3}) \times (4 \times 10^2)$

㊷ $(4.2 \times 10^{-3}) \div (7 \times 10^{-1})$

㊸ $(-8.6 \times 10^{-4}) \div (4 \times 10^2)$

㊹ $(1.25 \times 10^5) \div (5 \times 10^{-2})$

㊺ $(4.5 \times 10^{-2}) \times (-2.5 \times 10^6)$

㊻ $(8.1 \times 10^5) \div (9 \times 10^{-3})$

Answer the questions.

㊼ Express the numbers in scientific notation.

    a. 0.3   b. $\dfrac{1}{4}$ c. 10^2

    d. 3^5 e. 5^4 f. 2^{-3}

㊽ Arrange the following numbers in scientific notation from smallest to greatest.

    5.07×10^{-3}, -1.2×10^4, -3.4×10^{-1}, 8.9×10^2

㊾ Consider two numbers written in scientific notation in the form of $a \times 10^n$. Determine whether each statement is true or false. Justify your answer.

    a. The number that has a greater value of a must be greater.

    b. The number with the greater value of n in its power of 10 must be greater.

㊿ Why is writing numbers with powers of 10 more practical than with powers of other numbers? Give an example.

㈤ The volume of Earth is approximately 1.1×10^{12} km^3 and the volume of the moon is 2.2×10^{10} km^3. About how many times the volume of the moon is Earth's volume?

㈤ A virus particle is about 9×10^{-6} cm in diameter. An oxygen molecule has an approximate size of 3×10^{-8} cm. About how many times is a virus particle as large as an oxygen molecule?

㈤ In 2019, the GDP of Canada was \$1 712 429 million and the GDP per capita (meaning GDP per person) was \$46 290. Estimate the population of Canada in 2019 using scientific notation.

㈤ A light year is the distance light travels in one year, which is about 9.461×10^{12} km.

    a. Estimate the speed of light in m/s.

    b. The distance between Earth and the sun is about 148.4 million km. About how long does it take for light to travel from the sun to Earth?

㈤ The changes to a company's market value for the previous four quarters are listed in order: \$3.25 million, $\$2.04 \times 10^5$, $-\$1.2 \times 10^6$, and -\$845 000. What was the average change of the market value per quarter?

Things I have learned in this chapter:

- the composition of numbers in exponential notation
- applying the laws of exponents
- performing operations on powers
- relating square roots to squares and evaluating them
- writing numbers in scientific notation and performing operations on them

My Notes:

_____

_____

_____

_____

_____

_____

_____

_____

_____

_____

Chapter 2

Quiz 2

Knowledge and Understanding

Circle the correct answers.

① What does "3" in "2^3" represent?

    A. power   B. exponent

    C. base   D. reciprocal

② Which of the following is not a law of exponent?

    A. $a^m \times a^n = a^{m+n}$ B. $(a^m)^n = a^{mn}$

    C. $\left(\dfrac{a}{b}\right)^m = \dfrac{a^m}{b^m}$ D. $(a+b)^2 = a^2 + 2ab + b^2$

③ What does the identity exponent state?

    A. $a^0 = 1$ B. $a^1 = a$

    C. $(-a)^m = (-1)^m \times a^m$ D. $a^{-m} = \dfrac{1}{a^m}$

④ Which of the following is not in simplest form?

    A. $3\sqrt{5}$ B. $2\sqrt{8}$

    C. $4\sqrt{6}$ D. $-\sqrt{10}$

⑤ Which is not written in scientific notation correctly?

    A. 3.9×10^3 B. 0.6×10^{-2}

    C. -2.74×10^{-4} D. 1.008×10^5

⑥ Which power has a negative value?

    A. 2^{-4} B. $(-2)^4$

    C. $(-2)^{-4}$ D. -2^4

⑦ Which is the smallest?

    A. $\sqrt{300}$ B. 5^2

    C. 4^2 D. $\sqrt{289}$

Read the statements. Circle "T" for true and "F" for false.

⑧ Consider two powers with the same positive integer as their bases.   T / F
The power that has a greater exponent must be greater.

⑨ If two powers have the same exponent, the one with a negative   T / F
integer as its base must be smaller than the one with a positive integer
as its base.

⑩ In scientific notation, a negative exponent in the power of 10 means   T / F
that the number is negative.

⑪ The square root of a prime number is in its simplest form.   T / F

⑫ Consider a and b as integers.

   a. $(-a)^2$ can be evaluated but $\sqrt{(-a)^2}$ cannot.   T / F

   b. a^b must be positive if $b > 0$.   T / F

   c. a^b must be a perfect square if b is a positive even number.   T / F

Write each number as a product of powers using factor trees.

⑬   72 = _____   ⑭   225 = _____

⑮   196 = _____   ⑯   675 = _____

Write each as a single power.

⑰ $2^3 \times 2^5$ = _____

⑱ $(-3)^4 \div (-3)^2$ = _____

⑲ $5^3 \times 5^2 \div 5^4$ = _____

⑳ $(-2)^2 \times (-2)$ = _____

㉑ $8^{-4} \div 8^0 \times 8^3$ = _____

㉒ $(-7)^6 \times (-7)^{-1} \div (-7)^2$ = _____

㉓ $3^3 \times 9^2 \div 3^{-1}$ = _____

㉔ $10^3 \div 100^2 \times 1000^{-1}$ = _____

㉕ $(2^3)^2 \times 2^{-4}$ = _____

㉖ $3^4 \div (3^2)^3 \times 3$ = _____

㉗ $(5^2)^2 \times (25^2)^2$ = _____

㉘ $(6^{-1})^2 \div 36^{-1}$ = _____

Write each number as a power with a positive exponent.

㉙ 16 _____

㉚ 1000 _____

㉛ -27 _____

㉜ $(3^2)^4$ _____

㉝ $(5^3)^{-3}$ _____

㉞ $(6^{-2})^5$ _____

㉟ $\left(\dfrac{3}{5}\right)^{-2}$ _____

㊱ 11^{-3} _____

㊲ $\left(\dfrac{7}{6}\right)^{-3}$ _____

㊳ $\sqrt{16}$ _____

㊴ 3.43×10^2 _____

㊵ 1.25×10^{-1} _____

Evaluate and write the answers in simplest form. Show your work.

㊶ $3^5 \times 3^2 \div 3^3$

㊷ $4^3 \div 4^{-1} \times 4^6$

㊸ $2^{-6} \div 2^{-2} \times 8$

㊹ $(-6)^2 \times (6^3)^2$

㊺ $3^3 \times \dfrac{1}{9} \div 3^4$

㊻ $5^3 \div (5^{-2})^{-1} \times \dfrac{1}{25}$

47 $\dfrac{1.2^2}{3^2}$

48 $\sqrt{24} \times \sqrt{6}$

49 $\sqrt{200} \div \sqrt{10}$

50 $4\sqrt{2} \div \sqrt{8}$

51 $\dfrac{2\sqrt{16} \times 3\sqrt{2}}{2^2 \times \sqrt{2}}$

52 $\dfrac{2\sqrt{15} \times \sqrt{10}}{\sqrt{2} \times 3\sqrt{27}}$

Application

Solve the problems. Show your work.

53 A computer hard drive has 2^6 GB of memory and is divided into four sections. How many files that are 2^{-4} GB each can one section store? Write your answer as a power.

54 A rectangular rug has an area of 30 m². Its width is $3\sqrt{2}$ m. What is the length of the rug? Give an exact answer.

55 A movie earned $\$9.2 \times 10^8$ at the box office. On average, it earned $\$5.75 \times 10^6$ each day. How many days was the movie at the box office?

(56) The mass of Earth is approximately 5.972×10^{24} kg.

a. If all the nickel on Earth weighs 1.07496×10^{23} kg, what percent of Earth's mass comes from nickel?

b. If 30% of Earth's mass is from oxygen, how much does the oxygen on Earth weigh?

(57) A right triangle has a hypotenuse that measures $\sqrt{5}$ cm and a side that measures $\frac{3}{\sqrt{2}}$ m. What is the length of the third side? Give an exact answer.

(58) A square piece of paper has a side length of 2^4 cm. The paper is folded in half 6 times. What is the area of each small square formed?

Communication

Answer the questions.

(59) Describe how you write a number in scientific notation.

60 Use the product of powers to show the zero exponent ($a^0 = 1$ for $a \neq 0$).

61 Use the quotient of powers to show the identity exponent ($a^1 = a$).

62 Explain why a squared number cannot be negative.

Thinking

Find the answers.

63 Evaluate using the square root rules.

a. $\sqrt{\sqrt{256}}$

b. $\sqrt{4^3}$

c. $(\sqrt{800} \div 5)^{-2}$

64 Consider a as an integar where $a > 1$. Explain how you know that the value of the expression $(a^6)^2 \times (a^3)^{-5}$ is less than 1.

Chapter 3

Algebra

3.1 Algebraic Expressions

Key Ideas

Algebraic expressions are math expressions that have variables. These variables represent numerical values. Learning to simplify algebraic expressions is important and it is beneficial to simplify algebraic expressions before evaluating them. There are some principles to follow when simplifying algebraic expressions.

- clearing the brackets by multiplication/ division or exponent rules

- combining numbers and variables

Examples

$3(2x)$
$= 6x$ ←— clearing brackets by multiplication

$(x^2)^3$
$= x^6$ ←— clearing brackets by exponent rules

$2x + 4 + 7$
$= 2x + 11$ ←— combining numbers

$2x + x$
$= 3x$ ←— combining variables

Try these!

Fill in the blanks.

① Clearing Brackets

a. $5(2x) = \boxed{}\, x$

b. $2(8x^2) = \boxed{}\, x^2$

c. $\dfrac{1}{4}(4x) = \boxed{}\, x$

d. $(x^3)^3 = x^{\boxed{}}$

e. $(x^5)^{-1} = x^{\boxed{}}$

f. $-(x^2)^{-1} = -x^{\boxed{}}$

g. $4(x^2)^2 = \boxed{}\, x$

h. $-x^2(3x) = \boxed{}\, x$

② Combining Numbers

a. $x + 8 - 3 = x + \boxed{}$

b. $x - 10 + 4 = x - \boxed{}$

c. $10 - x + 6 = -x + \boxed{}$

d. $3 + x - 8 = x - \boxed{}$

e. $-2 - x - 1 = -x - \boxed{}$

f. $8 + x^2 - 5 = x^2 + \boxed{}$

g. $1 + x^2 - 2 = x^2 - \boxed{}$

h. $-5 - x^2 + 12 = -x^2 + \boxed{}$

③ Combining Variables

a. $2x + 3x = \boxed{}\, x$

b. $5x + x = \boxed{}\, x$

c. $9x - 2x = \boxed{}\, x$

d. $-x + 3x = \boxed{}\, x$

e. $3x^2 + x^2 = \boxed{}\, x^2$

f. $6x^2 - 4x^2 = \boxed{}\, x^2$

g. $8x^3 - x^3 = \boxed{}\, x^3$

h. $-2x^3 + 4x^3 = \boxed{}\, x^3$

Simplify the algebraic expressions.

④ $3(4x)$ = _____

⑤ $-2(8x)$ = _____

⑥ $(x^3)^2$ = _____

⑦ $x + 4x$ = _____

⑧ $5x^3 + x^3$ = _____

⑨ $7(x^2)^2$ = _____

⑩ $-2(x^2)^{-1}$ = _____

⑪ $-3x + 4x$ = _____

⑫ $x + 8 - 2$ = _____

⑬ $-x^2 + 4x^2$ = _____

⑭ $12(0.5x)$ = _____

⑮ $10 - x^2 + 5$ = _____

⑯ $0.4(10x)$ = _____

⑰ $2x + (-x)$ = _____

⑱ $-3 + x^3 + 1$ = _____

Simplify the algebraic expressions. Show your work.

⑲ $3(2x + x)$

⑳ $x(3x - x)$

Hint

Some useful laws and rules to remember when simplifying.

$$a^m \times a^n = a^{m+n}$$
$$a^m \div a^n = a^{m-n}$$
$$(a^m)^n = a^{mn}$$
$$(ab)^m = a^m b^m$$
$$\sqrt{a} \times \sqrt{a} = a$$
$$\sqrt{a^2} = a$$
$$\sqrt{ab} = \sqrt{a} \times \sqrt{b}$$
$$\sqrt{\frac{a}{b}} = \frac{\sqrt{a}}{\sqrt{b}}$$

㉑ $x(x^2)$

㉒ $5x(x^3)$

㉓ $-6(2x + 2x)$

㉔ $x(2x)(3x^2)$

㉕ $2x(4x - 3x)$

㉖ $\sqrt{x^2}\,(2x - x)$

㉗ $(x^2)^{-1}(2x^2 - x^2)$

㉘ $(x^2)^2(2x)^2$

㉙ $\sqrt{9x^2}(3x)^2$

㉚ $(x^2)^3(x + 2x)$

Evaluate each expression by substitution. Show your work.

③① Evaluate for $x = 2$.

    a. $4x$ b. $-8 \div x$

    c. x^2 d. $x^3 - 1$

Hint

Substitution is the process of replacing the variable in an algebraic expression with a numerical value.

e.g. Evaluate $x^2 - 1$ for $x = 3$.

$\quad\quad 3^2 - 1$ ← substitution

$\quad\quad = 9 - 1$

$\quad\quad = 8$

③② Evaluate for $x = -1$.

    a. $7x$ b. $x^3 + 1$ c. $-(x^2) - 6$

③③ Evaluate for $x = -2$.

    a. $2x^2$ b. $(\sqrt{-2x})^2$ c. $x^2(x + 3)$

Evaluate. Show your work.

③④ Evaluate $4x^2$.

    a. for $x = 1$ b. for $x = 3$

Hint

A variable can take on different numerical values.

e.g. Evaluate $x^2 + 1$.
- for $x = 2$
  $\quad 2^2 + 1 = 5$
- for $x = -1$
  $\quad (-1)^2 + 1 = 2$

③⑤ Evaluate $3(x^2)^3$.

    a. for $x = 2$ b. for $x = -1$ c. for $x = -2$

Evaluate the expressions with the given values. Show your work.

㉟ $x = 3$ $y = -1$

a. $2x + 3y$

b. $-4(x^2 + y)$

㊲ $a = 10$ $b = -2$

a. $a - b^2$

b. $(a^2b)^3$

㊳ $m = -3$ $n = 4$

a. $4m + n$

b. $6(m^2 - \sqrt{n})$

Simplify each algebraic expression. Then evaluate it with the given value. Show your work.

㊴ $2(4x - x)$ for $x = 3$

Hint

Simplifying an algebraic expression before evaluating it makes calculations easier.

e.g. $3x(x - 4x)$
= $3x(-3x)$ for $x = 2$
= $-9x^2$ → $-9(2^2) = -36$

㊵ $x(-x + 6x)$ for $x = -3$

㊶ $2x^2(x^3)$ for $x = -2$

㊷ $(x + x)(2x - x)$ for $x = 5$

㊸ $(-x + 2x)^2(x^2 + 2x^2)$ for $x = 2$

Answer the questions about the scenarios.

(44) Nathan worked x hours on Monday and 3 more than twice the hours on Tuesday.

a. Write an algebraic expression to show

- the number of hours Nathan worked on Tuesday. ____________
- the total number of hours Nathan worked. ____________

b. How many hours did Nathan work in total

- for $x = 1$? ____________
- for $x = 3$? ____________

(45) A small square has a side length of x cm and a big square's side length is triple that of the small square.

a. Write an algebraic expression to show the total area of the squares. ____________

b. What is the total area if

- $x = 2$? ____________
- $x = 5$? ____________

(46) For the scenarios above, can the values of x be less than 0? Explain.

____

____

For each statement, write "T" for true and "F" for false.

(47) For any algebraic expression, a variable can always take on only one numerical value. ______

(48) For algebraic expressions that have more than one variable, swapping their numerical values when evaluating will not change the answers. ______

(49) The numerical values of different variables must be different. ______

(50) A variable may take on different numerical values. ______

(51) Any variable may only take on integers as numerical values. ______

Answer the questions.

⑫ Simplify the algebraic expressions.

a. $(a^2)(a^2)$ b. $3x^3(x^5)$

c. $(3y)^2$ d. $(4n^2)^2$

e. $2(i + 2i)$ f. $-a(3a)(2a^2)$

g. $(6s - s)(s - 2s)$ h. $m^3(-m + 3m)$

⑬ Evaluate each expression with the given value.

a. $(b^2)^3$, for $b = -1$ b. $a^2 - 5$, for $a = 2$

c. $x^3 + x$, for $x = -2$ d. $k^2 - 2k$, for $k = 5$

e. $(-y^2)^{-1}$, for $y = -3$ f. 10^n, for $n = -2$

g. $i^2(i + 1)$, for $i = 0$ h. $d^d - d$, for $d = -3$

⑭ Simplify and then evaluate.

a. $\dfrac{(x^2)^3}{(x^2)^2}$, for $x = 4$ b. $\left(\dfrac{b^3}{b^5}\right)^{-2}$, for $b = 3$

c. $m(2m^2 - 5m^2)$, for $m = 2$ d. $\left(\dfrac{a}{a^{-2}}\right)\left(\dfrac{a^{-2}}{a^{10}}\right)$, for $a = -2$

⑮ Eva and Howard evaluated $10 - x^2$ for $x = -2$. Whose solution is correct? Point out the error for the incorrect one.

Eva's solution: $10 - (-2)^2$ Howard's solution: $10 - (-2^2)$

$= 10 - 4$ $= 10 - (-4)$

$= 6$ $= 14$

⑯ Explain why $\dfrac{a^2}{a - 2b}$ cannot be evaluated to a number for $a = 5$ and $b = 2.5$.

⑰ The surface area of a cube is $6s^2$ square centimentres where s is the side length in centimetres. Find the surface area for each value of s.

a. $s = 10$ b. $s = 45$ c. $s = 2.4$

⑱ The area of a circle is πr^2 where r is the radius and π is approximately equal to 3.14. If the radius of a circle is 6.2 cm, what is its area?

⑲ A rectangular prism has a length of x^3, a width of $3x$, and a height of $\dfrac{1}{4x^2}$.

a. Write a simplified algebraic expression to represent its volume.

b. Evaluate the volume for $x = 6$.

Chapter 3

3.2 Algebraic Equations

Key Ideas

All equations have two sides – the left-hand side (LHS) and the right-hand side (RHS). Our goal in solving an equation is to isolate the variable while maintaining equality. This means that what is done to one side must also be done to the other side. When solving an equation, perform the operation in reverse BEDMAS order.

Reverse BEDMAS Order

Addition/Subtraction

Multiplication/Division

Exponents

Brackets

In an equation that is solved, it is common practice to put the variable on the LHS of the equation and its value on the RHS.

Examples

$$3x + 1 = 13 \quad \longleftarrow \text{goal: isolating } x$$
$$3x + 1 - 1 = 13 - 1 \quad \longleftarrow \text{Perform subtraction first to eliminate "1".}$$
$$3x = 12$$
$$3x \div 3 = 12 \div 3 \quad \longleftarrow \text{Divide to eliminate "3".}$$
$$x = 4$$

$$\frac{(x-2)}{3} = 1 \quad \longleftarrow \text{Eliminate "3" before the brackets.}$$
$$\frac{(x-2)}{3} \times 3 = 1 \times 3 \quad \longleftarrow \text{Multiply to eliminate "3".}$$
$$x - 2 = 3$$
$$x - 2 + 2 = 3 + 2 \quad \longleftarrow \text{Add to eliminate "2".}$$
$$x = 5$$

Try these!

Fill in the blanks to solve the equations.

① $x + 10 = 15$

$x + 10 - 10 = 15 - \boxed{}$

$x = \boxed{}$

② $\frac{x}{4} = 9$

$\frac{x}{4} \times 4 = 9 \times \boxed{}$

$x = \boxed{}$

③ $2x - 1 = 11$

$2x - 1 + 1 = 11 + \boxed{}$

$2x = \boxed{}$

$2x \div 2 = \boxed{} \div \boxed{}$

$x = \boxed{}$

④ $\frac{x}{6} - 2 = 1$

$\frac{x}{6} - 2 + 2 = 1 + \boxed{}$

$\frac{x}{6} = \boxed{}$

$\frac{x}{6} \times 6 = \boxed{} \times 6$

$x = \boxed{}$

⑤ $2 + 3x = 8$

$2 + 3x - 2 = 8 - \boxed{}$

$3x = \boxed{}$

$3x \div 3 = \boxed{} \div \boxed{}$

$x = \boxed{}$

⑥ $2(x - 1) = 6$

$2(x - 1) \div 2 = 6 \div \boxed{}$

$x - 1 = \boxed{}$

$x - 1 + 1 = \boxed{} + \boxed{}$

$x = \boxed{}$

Solve the equations. Show your work.

⑦ $4x - 2 = 10$

⑧ $9 + 2x = 15$

⑨ $3(x - 2) = 9$

⑩ $\dfrac{2x}{3} = 8$

⑪ $\dfrac{x + 1}{4} = 6$

⑫ $5x - 3 = -8$

⑬ $-2(x + 3) = -10$

⑭ $\dfrac{4}{5}x + 6 = -2$

⑮ $-\dfrac{x + 1}{3} = 1$

⑯ $10 - 3x = 4$

⑰ $\sqrt{x} + 1 = 3$

Hint

The opposite of square root is squaring. Therefore, square a value to remove its square root.

e.g. $\sqrt{x} = 3$
$(\sqrt{x})^2 = 3^2$
$x = 9$

⑱ $2\sqrt{x} = 6$

⑲ $\dfrac{\sqrt{x} - 1}{5} = 1$

⑳ $3\sqrt{x} - 2 = 10$

Write an equation for each description. Then solve for x.

㉑ 5 less than the double of x is 3.

㉒ Tripling the sum of x and 1 is 9.

㉓ The sum of 4 and two third of x is 8.

㉔ One fourth of the sum of 6 and x is 2.

㉕ The triple of x subtracted from 7 is -2.

㉖ The product of -2 and the difference of x minus 1 is -6.

㉗ The sum of 10 and the square root of x is 13.

㉘ The sum of the square root of x and 9 is 13.

㉙ One fifth of the square root of x is 1.

㉚ The square root of the product of 2 and x is 4.

Answer the questions.

㉛ Solve for x.

a. $6x + 1 = 25$

b. $3(9 - x) = 15$

c. $\frac{3}{4}x + 1 = 7$

d. $-4(5 - x) = -24$

e. $\frac{8 - x}{2} = 5$

f. $-3(x + 7) = 9$

㉜ Solve for y.

a. $\sqrt{y} + 6 = 8$

b. $\sqrt{y} - 4 = -1$

c. $-6\sqrt{y} = -12$

d. $2\sqrt{y} + 1 = 21$

e. $-\sqrt{y} + 5 = 0$

f. $-8\sqrt{y} = -16$

㉝ Simplify the expression on the left side of each equation. Then solve.

a. $2x - 5 + x = 1$

b. $10 + 6x - 2 = -4$

c. $\frac{10(x - 9)}{5} = -8$

d. $(\sqrt{3x})^2 + 2 = 3$

e. $\sqrt{4x^2} + x + 4 = 13$

f. $(5\sqrt{x})^2 - 10x = 3$

㉞ Solve for the unknowns.

a. $\frac{x}{2} = \frac{4}{8}$

b. $\frac{7}{x} = \frac{2}{3}$

c. $\frac{x + 2}{10} = \frac{6}{5}$

d. $\frac{10}{3} = \frac{5}{x - 1}$

e. $\frac{x + 3}{8} = \frac{15}{4}$

f. $\frac{x \div 2}{5} = \frac{7}{10}$

g. $\frac{3}{x - 2} = \frac{5}{8}$

h. $\frac{6}{x \div 3} = \frac{-4}{5}$

Hint

Cross-multiply to rearrange an equation. Then solve.

e.g. $\frac{x}{4} = \frac{1}{2}$

$2x = 4$

$x = 2$

㉟ The students tried to solve $\sqrt{4x} + 1 = 5$. Their solutions are shown below. Whose solution is incorrect? Point out the error and write the correct solution.

• Dave's solution: $\sqrt{4x} + 1 = 5$

$\sqrt{4x} = 4$

$\sqrt{x} = 1$

$x = 1$

• Tom's solution: $\sqrt{4x} + 1 = 5$

$4x + 1 = 25$

$4x = 24$

$x = 6$

㊱ Elle says, "There is exactly one solution for $4(x + 1) = -8$." Is she correct? Explain.

㊲ Jacob says, "There is exactly one solution for $x^2 + 2 = 11$." Is he correct? Explain.

㊳ An equation with two or more variables has many solutions. Explain why this is true with an example.

Chapter 3

3.3 Problem Solving Using Algebra (1)

Key Ideas

As you have learned, an equation represents two expressions that are equal. A formula is an equation that states a fact or rule. It has an equal sign and two or more variables which are related to each other.

$x + y = 10$ ← a formula; relating x and y

$x + 2 = -1$ ← an equation; not a formula

With sufficient information, an unknown value can be found using a formula.

Examples

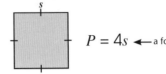

$P = 4s$ ← a formula

• Solve for s if $P = 20$.

$$20 = 4s$$ ← substituting 20 for P

$$20 \div 4 = 4s \div 4$$

$$s = 5$$ ← value of s

• Solve for s if $P = 10$.

$$10 = 4s$$ ← substituting 10 for P

$$10 \div 4 = 4s \div 4$$

$$s = 2.5$$ ← value of s

Fill in the blanks to solve for the unknowns. Show your work.

Try these!

① 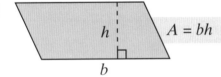 $A = bh$

a. Solve for h if $A = 35$ and $b = 5$.

$$35 = \boxed{}\; h$$

b. Solve for b if $A = 14$ and $h = 3.5$.

$$\boxed{} = 3.5b$$

c. Solve for A if $b = 8$ and $h = 2.5$.

$$A = (\boxed{})(2.5)$$

②  $P = 2(l + w)$

a. Solve for l if $P = 30$ and $w = 6$.

$$30 = 2(l + \boxed{})$$

b. Solve for w if $P = 21$ and $l = 7$.

$$\boxed{} = 2(7 + w)$$

c. Solve for P if $l = 10$ and $w = 0.25$.

$$P = 2(10 + \boxed{})$$

Write the formulas. Then solve for the indicated unknowns using algebra.

③ Area of a Triangle:

_____

a. Solve for h if $A = 20$ and $b = 4$.

b. Solve for b if $A = 16$ and $h = 8$.

④ 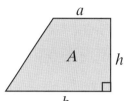 Area of a Trapezoid:

_____

a. Solve for a if $A = 9$, $b = 4$, and $h = 3$.

b. Solve for h if $A = 15$, $a = 2.5$, and $b = 5$.

⑤ Circumference of a Circle:

_____

a. Solve for r if $C = 18.84$.

b. Solve for C if $r = 2.5$.

⑥ 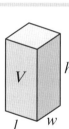 Volume of a Prism:

_____

a. Solve for l if $V = 112$, $w = 4$, and $h = 7$.

b. Solve for h if $V = 48$, $l = 5$, and $w = 1.2$.

Check the equation that represents each scenario. Then solve it.

⑦ There are 2 orders of m muffins and an order of 5 muffins for a total of 17 muffins. What is m?

○ $2m + 5 = 17$ ○ $2(m + 5) = 17$

⑧ The regular price of a light bulb is $\$p$. The total cost for 4 of them at $1 off each is $26. What is p?

○ $4p - 1 = 26$ ○ $4(p - 1) = 26$

⑨ It was t°C one day in Vancouver. The temperature in Montreal was -10°C, which was 1°C more than twice that in Vancouver. What is t?

○ $2t + 10 = 1$ ○ $2t + 1 = -10$

⑩ A regular box has d doughnuts and a value-sized one has 2 more. If one third of a value-sized box has 4 doughnuts, what is d?

○ $\dfrac{(d + 2)}{3} = 4$ ○ $\dfrac{d}{3} + 2 = 4$

⑪ There were c cartons in the fridge. Half of them are sold and after restocking 6 cartons, there are 21 cartons. What is c?

○ $\dfrac{c + 6}{2} = 21$ ○ $\dfrac{c}{2} + 6 = 21$

⑫ The number of eggs to bananas for a recipe is 6:5. If 2 eggs and 10 bananas are added, how many more eggs, e, are needed?

○ $\dfrac{6}{5} = \dfrac{2 + e}{10}$ ○ $\dfrac{6}{5} = \dfrac{e}{10} + 2$

⑬ A square has an area of a cm^2 and a perimeter of 36 cm. What is a?

○ $4\sqrt{a} = 36$ ○ $4a^2 = 36$

⑭ Customers get 1 free doughnut for every 6 doughnuts bought. A company buys d dozen doughnuts and got 8 free doughnuts. What is d?

○ $\dfrac{6}{12d} = \dfrac{8}{1}$ ○ $\dfrac{1}{6} = \dfrac{8}{12d}$

Answer the questions.

⑮ The formula that relates Celsius (C) and Fahrenheit (F) is $C = \dfrac{5}{9}(F - 32)$. Convert the temperatures.

a. 212°F
b. 32°F
c. -13°F

d. 35°C
e. 70°C
f. -5°C

⑯ Consider the formulas below.

Hint

- $A = \boldsymbol{l}w$; $A = 55$, $w = 2.2$

- $P = 2(l + \boldsymbol{w})$; $P = 16$, $l = \dfrac{3}{8}$

- $A = \dfrac{b\boldsymbol{h}}{2}$; $A = \sqrt{15}$, $h = \sqrt{6}$

- $C = 2\pi\boldsymbol{r}$; $C = 0.0628$

- $V = \pi r^2\boldsymbol{h}$; $V = 157$, $r = 10$

a. Rearrange the terms in each formula to make the variable in bold the subject of the formula.

b. Solve for each subject using the given values.

> The subject of a formula is a variable that is expressed in terms of other variables and/or numerical values in the formula. This single variable is usually on the left-hand side of a formula.
>
> $S = \dfrac{d}{t}$ Speed (S) is distance (d)
> ↑   over time (t).
> subject

⑰ Michael and Allen each set up an equation for this scenario:

A 34-unit-long frill was to be sewed around a square blanket with an area of a square units. If 10 units of the frill was not used, what is a?

Michael's solution:
$$4\sqrt{a} + 10 = 34$$
$$4\sqrt{a} = 24$$
$$4a = 576$$
$$a = 144$$

Allen's solution:
$$4a^2 + 10 = 34$$
$$4a^2 = 24$$
$$a^2 = 6$$
$$a = \sqrt{6}$$

However, neither of the solutions is correct. Describe the errors they made and write the correct solution.

Celsius and Fahrenheit – these two measuring units are commonly used to measure temperature. What makes these two units different are their reference points. The Celsius scale, created by Andres Celsius, is in the metric system where its reference points were set to be the freezing point of water at 0°C and the boiling point of water at 100°C. How about Fahrenheit? What are its reference points? Other than temperatures in °C and °F, there are also the Kelvin Scale and the Rankine Scale. Scan the QR code to learn more.

Chapter 3

3.4 Problem Solving Using Algebra (2)

Key Ideas

Although it might seem intimidating at first, setting up algebraic equations for problem solving only requires applying simple concepts. It will eventually become a lot easier through practice and following the key steps below to set up equations before solving them.

Steps to Solve Problems Using Algebra

❶ Let a variable represent the unknown or the value you are trying to solve for.

❷ Set up an equation using the given information such that both sides of the equation are equal.

❸ Solve for the variable by manipulating the equation.

Examples

Half of the apples on a tree were picked and another 10 of them dropped to the ground. There are 35 apples left on the tree. How many apples were there on the tree?

Let x be the number of apples there were on the tree. ←❶

$$\frac{x}{2} - 10 = 35 \quad \text{←❷}$$
$$\frac{x}{2} - 10 + 10 = 35 + 10$$
$$\frac{x}{2} = 45$$
$$\frac{x}{2} \times 2 = 45 \times 2$$
$$x = 90 \quad \text{←❸}$$

There were 90 apples on the tree.

Fill in the blanks to set up the equations and solve them.

Try these!

① Ted walks at a speed of 3.5 km/h. How long will it take him to walk 10.5 km?

Let x be the amount of time it will take.

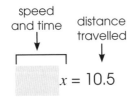

speed and time   distance travelled

$$\boxed{}\,x = 10.5$$

It will take Ted [ ] h.

↑ value of x

② Jon paid for 12 muffins using a $50-bill and got $13.40 in change. How much was each muffin?

Let x be the cost of each muffin.

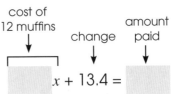

cost of 12 muffins   change   amount paid

$$\boxed{}\,x + 13.4 = \boxed{}$$

The cost of each muffin was $ [ ] .

↑ value of x

Set up an equation to solve each problem algebraically.

③ A leak drips water at 8 mL/min. How long will it take a pail to be filled with 400 mL of dripping water?

Let x be _____ .

④ Lee made a $1560 down payment for a new car which was 13% of the car's price. What was the car's price?

⑤ Carol used a 20%-off coupon to save $3 from her bill. How much was the original bill?

⑥ Hanna had 3 packs of batteries. She used 9 of them and has 15 batteries left. How many batteries were there in each pack?

⑦ A pancake recipe requires 3 cups of flour for $\frac{3}{4}$ cup of milk. How much milk is needed for 5 cups of flour?

⑧ Each travel-sized pack has 20 fewer towelettes than a regular pack. If there are 100 towelettes in 10 travel-sized packs, how many are there in a regular one?

⑨ 8 oak trees were added so that each side of a road has 25 trees. How many trees were there in total before the oak trees were added?

⑩ There are 50 dimes and some nickels in a jar that are worth a total of $6.25. How many nickels are there?

⑪ Mr. Grey had $40 in his wallet and he withdrew some money from a bank. If he spent $\frac{3}{4}$ of his money to buy a $75 shirt, how much did he withdraw?

⑫ On a road trip, Jeff drove $1\frac{1}{2}$ h at 60 km/h to reach his cottage. He drove 20% faster on his return trip. How long did the return trip take?

⑬ Jane wanted to put 210 beads equally into bags. However, 5 beads rolled off so the last bag has only 25 beads. How many bags of beads are there?

⑭ Kate used $\frac{3}{5}$ of the balance on a gift card and $25 to pay for a $55 humidifier. What was the balance on the gift card?

Answer the questions.

⑮ Determine the equation that is not equivalent to the rest in each set.

a. $x + 6 = 2y$

$x = 2y + 6$

$y = \dfrac{x + 6}{2}$

$6 = 2y - x$

b. $\dfrac{2x}{3} = y + 5$

$2x = 3(y + 5)$

$y = \dfrac{2x}{3} - 5$

$3x = \dfrac{y + 5}{2}$

Hint

Rearrange the terms in the equations so that they have the same subject. Then compare.

⑯ Set up an algebraic equation for each problem.

a. Danny paid $30 for 8 peaches and 10 plums at $1.80/plum. What was the unit price for peaches?

b. The perimeter of a square is 56 cm. What is its area?

c. Sarah invested $300 at an annual simple interest rate of 2%. How long will it take her to earn $36 in interest?

⑰ Solve each problem algebraically.

a. Justin had 7 bags of 10 marbles in assorted colours. He took out the same number of marbles from each bag for a craft and there are 49 marbles left. How many marbles did he take from each bag?

b. A rectangle has a length that doubles its width. Its perimeter is 48 cm. What is its width?

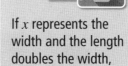

Hint

If x represents the width and the length doubles the width, then the length is $2x$.

c. A triangle has an area of 180 cm² with its height being 1.6 times its base.

• What is the measure of the base?

• What is the measure of the height?

d. Tony has a collection of quarters and dimes. There are 60 more dimes than quarters. The total value of the quarters and that of the dimes are the same. How many quarters and dimes does Tony have in his collection?

Things I have learned in this chapter:

• simplifying algebraic expressions

• evaluating algebraic expressions by substituting known values

• representing scenarios using algebraic expressions and equations

• solving equations

• solving word problems algebraically

• using formulas to find unknowns

My Notes:

_____

_____

_____

_____

_____

_____

_____

_____

_____

Chapter 3

Quiz 3

Knowledge and Understanding

Circle the correct answers.

① Which of the following is not an algebraic expression?

    A. $3x^2$ B. $10 - y$

    C. 5π D. $\sqrt{2a}$

② Which is the simplest form of $\dfrac{(x^2)(x^{-3})}{x}$?

    A. x^2 B. x^{-7}

    C. $\dfrac{x^{-1}}{x}$ D. x^{-2}

③ Which set of values of x and y for $3x - y$ will not give 4?

    A. $x = -1, y = -7$ B. $x = 3, y = 5$

    C. $x = 2, y = 2$ D. $x = 1, y = 1$

④ Which is the value of x in $\dfrac{4}{3}x = 12$?

    A. 6   B. 9

    C. 12   D. 16

⑤ Which equation represents $4:5 = x:9$?

    A. $\dfrac{4}{5} = \dfrac{9}{x}$ B. $\dfrac{4}{5} = \dfrac{x}{9}$

    C. $4 \times 5 = x \times 9$ D. $4 + 5 = x + 9$

⑥ Which algebraic expression is not equivalent to the others?

    A. $a = \dfrac{3}{2}(M - 5)$ B. $M = \dfrac{2}{3}(a - 5)$

    C. $3M = 2(a - 5)$ D. $a = \dfrac{3}{2}M + 5$

⑦ Which of the following is not a formula?

    A. $a + b = 7$ B. $2a^2 + a = 10$

    C. $\dfrac{4}{3}a = 5b$ D. $6b + 4 = a$

Simplify the expressions.

⑧ $2(8x)$ _____

⑨ $-3(7e)$ _____

⑩ $5(9c^2)$ _____

⑪ $-\dfrac{2}{5}(10a)$ _____

⑫ $(b^2)^3$ _____

⑬ $3(m^{-1})^3$ _____

⑭ $10c + 6c$ _____

⑮ $-4d + 8d$ _____

⑯ $7x^2 - 2x^2 + 9x^2$ _____

⑰ $\dfrac{4}{5}n^3 - \dfrac{3}{10}n^3 + \dfrac{1}{5}n^3$ _____

Simplify the algebraic expressions. Then evaluate them with the given values.

⑱ $4(c + 2c)$ $c = 1$

⑲ $2x(x^3)$ $x = 2$

⑳ $-7(-5n + 2n)$ $n = -2$

㉑ $(3p^2)^2$ $p = 3$

㉒ $(-2r^{-1})^3$ $r = -3$

㉓ $5y(y - 2y)$ $y = 10$

㉔ $-k^2(k^2 - 2k^2)$ $k = 3$

㉕ $\sqrt{4m^2}\,(2m)^2$ $m = \dfrac{1}{2}$

㉖ $(s^3)^{-2}(s + s)$ $s = -1$

Solve the equations. Show your work.

㉗ $4a + 1 = 9$

㉘ $\dfrac{2}{5}d - 4 = 0$

㉙ $-10 + 2k = -4$

㉚ $6(h - 1) = -12$

㉛ $\dfrac{4c}{9} = 8$

㉜ $\dfrac{2x + 1}{3} = -1$

㉝ $\dfrac{n}{9} = \dfrac{12}{4}$

㉞ $\dfrac{r + 1}{2} = \dfrac{5}{3}$

㉟ $5k - 11 = k + 13$

Write the formula for each. Then solve for the unknown with the given values.

㊱ 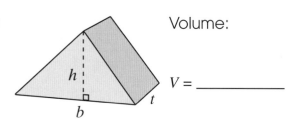 Volume:

$V =$ _____

Find t if $V = 60$, $b = 10$, and $h = 6$.

㊲ 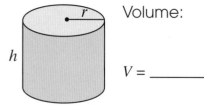 Volume:

$V =$ _____

Find h if $V = 127.17$ and $r = 3$.

Application

Find the answers.

㊳ Doris spends $$d$ each day for lunch. One day last week, she spent an extra $6 on a smoothie.

    a. Write an algebraic expression to show the total
       amount Doris spent on lunch last week.   _____

    b. How much did she spend if $d = 12$?   _____

㊴ A chef had 9 boiled eggs and then made e more boiled eggs. She used half of all boiled eggs to make an egg salad.

    a. Write an algebraic expression to show how
       many boiled eggs were used in the salad.   _____

    b. How many eggs were used if $e = 5$?   _____

Set up an equation to solve each problem algebraically. Show your work.

㊵ Last month, Ravi spent $135 on groceries which accounted for 30% of her spending. How much was her spending last month?

㊶ A delivery driver earns $3.50 on each order. One morning, including $22.50 of tips, he earned a total of $75. How many orders did he deliver?

㊷ Ivy chipped in $\frac{4}{5}$ of her savings and Ian chipped in $8 for their mother's gift, which cost $68. What was Ivy's savings?

㊸ A coin purse has nickels and quarters only with a total value of of $2.60. If there are 7 nickels, how many quarters are there?

㊹ The base of a triangle is twice its height. If the area of the triangle is 169 cm², what is its height?

Communication

Answer the questions.

㊺ Describe an advantage of simplifying an algebraic expression before evaluating it.

㊻ Consider $\dfrac{2}{(x-4)^2}$. What is the restriction on x? Why is this restriction important?

Thinking

Find the answers.

㊼ Solve for x. Show your work.

a. $\sqrt{2x-1}=9$

b. $\dfrac{8}{\sqrt{4x}}=\dfrac{\sqrt{x}}{5}$

c. $\dfrac{(\sqrt{x^2})^2+x^2}{x}=3x-1$

d. $\sqrt{x-\dfrac{1}{4}}=2\sqrt{5}$

e. $3\sqrt{x}=\dfrac{1}{2}\sqrt{x+1}$

f. $x(x-2)^2=\sqrt{x^2}\,(x-2)$

㊽ Solve the problems algebraically. Show your work.

a. Tony's cousin, Tanya, is 18 years older than Tony. This year, her age is four times that of Tony's. How old was Tony last year? Set up an equation to solve the problem.

b. A rectangle's length is twice its width and this width is the same as the side length of a square. If the rectangle's area is 25 cm² greater than the square's, what is the width of the rectangle? Set up an equation to solve the problem.

Polynomials

4.1 Introduction to Polynomials

Key Ideas

A polynomial is an algebraic expression that consists of one or more terms with exponents that are non-negative integers. These terms are separated by addition or subtraction. Monomials, binomials, and trinomials are all polynomials with specific number of terms.

- **monomial:**
  a polynomial with one term

- **binomial:**
  a polynomial with two terms

- **trinomial:**
  a polynomial with three terms

There are no specific names for polynomials that have four terms or more, and they are referred to as polynomials.

Examples

Circle the specified polynomials.

- **Monomials:**

  x $2x + 1$ 8 ← has 1 term

  $-x - 4$ x^2 $\dfrac{x}{2}$

- **Binomials:**

  $3x$ $x + 2$ -10 ← has 2 terms

  $x^2 + x$ $4x^2$ $-\dfrac{x}{2} - 1$

- **Trinomials:**

  $6x$ $2x^2 + x - 1$ $x - 1$ ← has 3 terms

  $3x^3 + 2x^2$ $x^2 - \dfrac{1}{4}x + 2$ $((x^2)^3)^{-1}$

Find the number of terms each polynomial has. Then write "M" for monomials, "B" for binomials, and "T" for trinomials.

Try these!

① $x + 2$

② $8x^2 - x + 4$

③ $4x - 1$

④ 10

⑤ $2x^2$

⑥ $-x^3 + x^2 - 1$

⑦ $x^2 - x + 3$

⑧ $x^2 + \dfrac{1}{2}$

⑨ $\dfrac{3}{5}x + \dfrac{1}{6}$

⑩ $-\dfrac{7}{10}x^3$

⑪ $(x^3)^2$

⑫ $6 + 4x$

⑬ $\dfrac{3}{4}x^2 + \dfrac{1}{3}x - 1$

⑭ 4^3

⑮ $-1 + x - \dfrac{1}{2}x^3$

Practice

Determine the degree of each term. Then determine the degree of each polynomial.

<table>
<tr><td></td><td>Degree of Polynomial</td></tr>
</table>

⑯

a. x^2 ⬆ _____

b. $2x^2 + x$ ⬆ ⬆ _____

c. $x^2y + x + xy + y^2$ ⬆ ⬆ ⬆ ⬆ _____

d. $-3x^2 + 4x^2y^2 - 5 + 2xy^4$ ⬆ ⬆ ⬆ ⬆ _____

e. $4x^3y + x^3y^3 - x^2y^2 - y$ ⬆ ⬆ ⬆ ⬆ _____

f. $-x^3y^2 + (x^2)^3y - 10$ ⬆ ⬆ ⬆ _____

> **Hint** 🔆
>
> The degree of a term refers to the sum of the exponents of the variables.
>
> e.g. Degree of $2x$: 1 ⬅ $x = x^1$
>
> Degree of x^2y: 3 ⬅ $2 + 1 = 3$
>
> Degree of 1: 0
>
> ─────────────
>
> The degree of a polynomial refers to the highest degree among the terms.
>
> e.g. $x^2y + x + 1$
> ⬆ ⬆ ⬆
> degree: 3   degree: 1   degree: 0
> (highest)
>
> Degree of polynomial: 3

Write whether each polynomial is a monomial, binomial, or trinomial. Then identify its degree.

⑰

	Monomial, Binomial, or Trinomial	Degree
a. $2x + 5$	_____	_____
b. $3x^2 - x$	_____	_____
c. $4x^2y + y$	_____	_____
d. $x^2 + 2xy - 5$	_____	_____
e. $10x^4$	_____	_____
f. $-\frac{1}{2}x^2y + x^3y - 6$	_____	_____
g. $(x^2)^2 + 2xy - xy^2$	_____	_____
h. $-x^4y - 10$	_____	_____

Circle the polynomials that match each description.

⑱ binomials of degree 2

    A. $4x^2 - x$

    B. $2x + y$

    C. x^2

    D. $-x^2 - 10$

⑲ trinomials of degree 3

    A. $x^3 + x + 5$

    B. $2x^3 - 1$

    C. $x^2 + 6x + 1$

    D. $-x^3 - 3x^2 - 8$

⑳ monomials of degree 3

    A. $x + y + z$

    B. $x^2 y$

    C. $2xy$

    D. xyz

㉑ polynomials of degree 4

    A. $4x^2 + 6y^2 - x - y$

    B. $x^2 y^2$

    C. $-3xy^4 + y^4$

    D. $1 - xy - xy^2 - x^3 y$

㉒ binomials of degree 3

    A. $xy^2 + x^2$

    B. $10 - 3x$

    C. $-x^2 y - y^3 - 4$

    D. $4xy^2 + x^2 y$

㉓ polynomials of degree 5

    A. $-2x^5 y$

    B. $x^2 y^2 z - 2xy$

    C. $x^3 + y^3 - x^2 + y^2 - 6$

    D. $-8x^2 y^3 - 1$

Rewrite the polynomials in standard form.

㉔ $6x + x^2$ _____

㉕ $10 + 2x^2 + x$ _____

㉖ $x - 3x^2 + 1$ _____

㉗ $x^3 + 5 - 2x^2$ _____

㉘ $12 - x^2 - 5x$ _____

㉙ $3x^2 + x^2 y + 7y$ _____

㉚ $y - xy^2 + y^2$ _____

㉛ $-xy - 9x + x^2 y$ _____

㉜ $5xy - x^3 + x^2 y^2$ _____

Hint

When a polynomial is written in standard form, it means the terms are ordered from the one with the highest degree to the one with the lowest.

e.g.

$$x - 2x^2 + 1 \implies -2x^2 + x + 1$$

Note that this term is $-2x^2$, not $2x^2$. So, remember to include the "-" when rearranging.

Answer the questions.

③③ For each polynomial, determine whether it is a monomial, binomial, or trinomial. Then find the degree of the polynomial.

a. $x^2 + 4$

b. $-y^3 + 4y + 9$

c. x^2yz^3

d. $-7x^2 + xy$

e. $-10xy^2$

f. $9y^3z - yz^2 + 4$

③④ Determine the degree of each polynomial and rewrite each one in standard form.

a. $3x^2 - 4 + x^4$

b. $-9 + 6x^3 - 5x$

c. $7x^2 - 4 + 6x^4 - x^3$

d. $10x^2y + 5y^2 - 2x^2y^2$

e. $-x^4 - 4x^2 + 3xy^2$

f. $-4a^3b + a^2b^3 + ab - 2ab^2$

g. $2x^2y - x^3y^2 + 4xy^3$

h. $3m^2n - 2n^4 + m^2n^3$

i. $3x^2y - 2y^2z^2 + 4x^2yz^2$

③⑤ Write your own polynomials with the given descriptions in standard form.

a. a binomial of degree 1

b. a trinomial of degree 4

c. a monomial of degree 3

d. a monomial of degree 3 with 2 variables

e. a binomial of degree 4

f. a binomial of degree 4 with 3 variables

③⑥ Determine whether each statement below is true or false.

a. A binomial must be a polynomial. So, a polynomial must also be a binomial.

b. The sum of three different variables must be a trinomial.

c. Any variable is a monomial by itself but a constant by itself cannot be a monomial.

d. A binomial cannot have a degree greater than 2.

e. A binomial must have a degree of 1 or greater.

f. For a polynomial in standard form, the term with the most variables is always the first term.

M A T H   I R L

Polynomials are an important tool used to represent and make sense of real-life scenarios and problems ranging from simple word problems to complicated scientific applications. For example, in the field of medication, a polynomial formula is used to calculate medicine dosage based on different variables of a patient, including weight, age, metabolism, and medical history. Scan this QR code to learn more about the application of polynomials in various fields.

Chapter 4

4.2 Adding and Subtracting Polynomials

Key Ideas

Polynomials, like numbers, can be added and subtracted. Before getting into adding and subtracting polynomials, you must learn to identify coefficients and like terms.

- **coefficient:**
  the factor by which a variable is multiplied

- **like terms:**
  algebraic terms that have the same variables and exponents

To add or subtract polynomials:

❶ Group the like terms.

❷ Add or subtract their coefficients.

Examples

Identify the coefficient of each term.

- $5x$ $\underline{\quad 5 \quad}$

- $-y$ $\underline{\quad -1 \quad}$ Coefficients can be any numbers that are positive or negative.

- $\frac{1}{2}x^2$ $\underline{\quad \frac{1}{2} \quad}$

- $0.7y^2$ $\underline{\quad 0.7 \quad}$

Circle the like terms in each set.

- $\boxed{x}$ $-x^2$ $\boxed{3x}$ ← common: x

- y^2 $\boxed{2y}$ $\boxed{-y}$ ← common: y

- $\boxed{x^2y}$ x^2 $\boxed{4x^2y}$ ← common: x^2y

Try these!

Fill in the blanks.

① Consider the terms below.

$$\frac{1}{4}y^3 \qquad 2x \qquad -3x^2y \qquad x^2y \qquad -xy \qquad 2x^2y^3 \qquad -3xy \qquad -x^2y^3 \qquad y^3 \qquad \frac{1}{4}x$$

   a. List the terms that have the specified coefficients.

- coefficient of 2:

- coefficient of -3:

- coefficient of $\frac{1}{4}$:

- coefficient of -1:

- coefficient of 1:

   b. List the terms that are like terms of the given ones.

- x:

- xy:

- x^2y:

- y^3:

- x^2y^3:

Circle the two like terms in each set. Then write another example that belongs to the set.

② x $-x^2$ xy $3x$

Example: _____

③ $2y$ y^2 $-5y$ $4xy$

Example: _____

④ a^2b $10a^2$ $-a^2$ ab

Example: _____

⑤ m^3 $3m^2n$ $2m^2$ m^2n

Example: _____

⑥ $4x^2y$ $-x^2y$ xy^2 $4xy$

Example: _____

⑦ $3x$ 16 -5 $2x^2$

Example: _____

Simplify each expression. Then write its coefficient in the box.

⑧ $3(2x)$ = _____

⑨ $-4(3y)$ = _____

⑩ $6(5x^2)$ = _____

⑪ $-2(7y^2)$ = _____

⑫ $\dfrac{1}{2}(4x^2y)$ = _____

⑬ $(3x)^2$ = _____

⑭ $(3x^2y)^2$ = _____

⑮ $-(x^2y^2)^3$ = _____

Add or subtract the like terms.

⑯ $4x + 5x$ = _____

⑰ $-3x + 6x$ = _____

⑱ $9y - 2y$ = _____

⑲ $y - 7y$ = _____

⑳ $x^2 + 2x^2$ = _____

㉑ $-5x^2 + 7x^2$ = _____

㉒ $-x^2 - 2x^2$ = _____

㉓ $-10y + 4y$ = _____

㉔ $2x - 3x + x$ = _____

㉕ $y - 6y + 4y$ = _____

㉖ $-x^2 + 5x^2 - x^2$ = _____

㉗ $5y^3 + y^3 - 6y^3$ = _____

㉘ $3xy + 6xy$ = _____

㉙ $-xy - xy$ = _____

㉚ $2xy^2 + xy^2$ = _____

㉛ $x^2y - 4x^2y + x^2y$ = _____

㉜ $xy^2 + 7xy^2 - 2xy^2$ = _____

㉝ $3x^3y - 5x^3y + 2x^3y$ = _____

> **Hint**
>
> Add or subtract the coefficients of the like terms.
>
> e.g. $2x + 3x = 5x$
> $2 + 3 = 5$
>
> $6x^2 - 2x^2 = 4x^2$
> $6 - 2 = 4$

Simplify each expression. Show your work.

㉞ $(x^2)^2 + 2x^4$

㉟ $-2x^3 + x(x^2)$

㊱ $(x^3)^2 + 2(x^2)^3$

㊲ $-(2x)^2 + 3x^2$

㊳ $(3x)^2 - (2x)^2$

㊴ $(2x^2)^2 - (-x)^4$

Hint

Simplify each term before adding or subtracting.

e.g. $(x^2)^2 + 5x^4$

$= x^4 + 5x^4$

$= 6x^4$

$2x^3 - x(x^2)$

$= 2x^3 - x^3$

$= x^3$

Add or subtract the like terms to simplify. Show your work.

㊵ $3x + (1 - x)$

㊶ $-x^2 + (-3x^2 + 5)$

㊷ $3x - (4x + 2)$

㊸ $-2y - (-5 - 2y)$

Hint

When removing the brackets of an expression for a subtraction, always remember to rewrite each term within the brackets with its opposite sign.

e.g. $7x - (x + 1)$

$= 7x - x - 1$

$= 6x - 1$

㊹ $(-x - 3) + (2 - 6x)$

㊺ $(-x^2 + 2x^2) + (-3 + x^2 - 2)$

㊻ $(2y - 4 - 3y) - (4y - 2)$

㊼ $(x^3 - 4) + (2 - x^3) - 5x^3$

Add and subtract to simplify the polynomials. Show your work.

㊽ $2x + 3y - x + 2y$ ㊾ $-7x - 4y - x + 6y$

Hint

Group the like terms
to add or subtract to simplify
polynomials.

e.g. $x + 3y + 2x - y$
$= x + 2x + 3y - y$
$= 3x + 2y$

㊿ $-x + 8 + 6x - 10$ 51 $x + 6x^2 - 4x^2 + 2x$

52 $(2x - 3y) + (x - 4y)$ 53 $(5x - y) - (2x - 3y)$ 54 $(3x - 2) + (2x - 8)$

55 $(-4x - 5) - (6x + 3)$ 56 $(xy + 5y) - (5xy - y)$ 57 $(x^2 + 2x) - (4x + 3x^2)$

58 $4x^2 - (3x + x^2) - 2x$ 59 $(x^2y + y) - (-y + x^2y)$ 60 $-y^2 - (4xy - y^2) + xy$

61 $7y^2 - (y^2 + 2y - 1)$ 62 $(-x^2 + 7x) - (2x + 1)$ 63 $(x^2 + 2xy) - (4xy - x)$

64   $(-2x^2y - y) + (3x^2 + y)$

65   $(2x^2 + x - 1) + (x^2 + 3x + 5)$

66   $(x^2 + 4x - 5) - (3x^2 + x - 2)$

67   $(2x^2 - xy + y^2) + (x^2 + 3xy - 2y^2)$

68   $(3x^2 + xy) + (xy - 2y^2) - (x^2 - y^2)$

69   $(2x^2 + 5) - (6x + 2) - (3x^2 + 4x)$

Fill in the blanks by adding and subtracting the polynomials.

70

Adding Polynomials		Sum
$3x + 5$		$5x + 8$
$4x^2 - 3x$		$5x^2 + x$
$2x^2 - x + 4$		$3x^2 + 5x - 1$
	$x^2 + 3x - 2$	$4x^2 - x + 3$

71

Subtracting Polynomials		Difference
$10x + 3$		$3x + 1$
$5x^2 - 3x$		$2x^2 + x$
$x^2 - 2x + 5$		$3x^2 - x$
	$x^2 + 5$	$3x^2 + 5x$

Answer the questions.

⑦² Find the coefficient of each term.

　a. $2x$　　　　　　b. $-3xy$　　　　　c. $\frac{1}{2}x^2$　　　　　d. $5(2x)$

　e. $0.3(10x)^2$　　f. $5x^2y$　　　　g. $(3x)^2$　　　　h. $(-6y)^2$

⑦³ Identify the like terms in each group.

　a. $-5x$, $3y$, $2.2x$, $-x$

　b. $5xy$, $-2xy^2$, $0.1xy^2$, $4xy^2$

　c. $2y^3$, $-y^3$, xy^3, $10y^3$

　d. $-6xy$, $-2x^2y$, $3xy$, $0.3xy$

　e. $-\frac{1}{5}x$, xy^3, $-5xy^3$, $\frac{1}{3}xy^3$

　f. $-1.25x^2y^2$, $(2x)^2y$, $(-xy)^2$, $3(xy)^2$

⑦⁴ Add or subtract the polynomials.

　a. $(3x + 2y) - (x + y)$

　b. $(5x^2 + 2x) + (x^2 - x)$

　c. $(-x^2 - 2y) - (3x^2 + 7y)$

　d. $(9y^2 + xy) + (8y^2 - 6xy)$

　e. $(2x^2 + 5x - 2) + (5x^2 - 2x)$

　f. $(4x - 2y + 4) - (x^3 + 2x + 1)$

　g. $(10 - x^2 + x^2y) + (-2x^2y - 4)$

　h. $(2x + 5y - 2) + (4x - 2xy) - (2y - 2)$

　i. $(xy^2 + 7xy) - (6xy^2 - xy + 2)$

　j. $(-5xy + 6x) - (6y + xy + 5) + (-2x - 3xy)$

⑦⁵ Determine whether each statement below is true or false.

　a. The sum of two trinomials is always a trinomial.

　b. The difference of two binomials cannot be a monomial.

　c. The sum of a monomial and a binomial can be a trinomial.

　d. The difference of two monomials cannot be a trinomial.

⑦⁶ A courier company charges a flat rate of $40 plus $5/kg of a parcel for regular delivery service and a flat rate of $55 plus $7/kg for express service.

　a. Write a polynomial to represent the delivery cost of regular service.

　b. Write a polynomial to represent the delivery cost of express service.

　c. Write a polynomial to represent how much more it costs to use the express service than the regular service.

　d. Calculate the difference in cost if a parcel weighs 8 kg.

Chapter 4

4.3 Multiplying Polynomials

Key Ideas

To determine the product of a monomial and a polynomial, apply the distributive property. According to the distributive property, when a sum is multiplied by a number, each value in the sum is multiplied by the number separately and their products are added.

Distributive Property

$$a(b + c) = ab + ac$$

e.g. $2 \times (3 + 4)$ $2 \times (3 + 4)$
        $= 2 \times 7$ $= 2 \times 3 + 2 \times 4$
        $= 14$ $= 6 + 8$
                $= 14$

Examples

$2(x + 3)$ ← multiplying each term in the binomial by 2

$= 2(x) + 2(3)$

$= 2x + 6$

$(x^2 + x - 2)4$ ← multiplying each term in the trinomial by 4

$= x^2(4) + x(4) - 2(4)$

$= 4x^2 + 4x - 8$

$x(2x + 5)$ ← multiplying each term in the binomial by x

$= x(2x) + x(5)$

$= 2x^2 + 5x$ ← applying exponential rule on $x(2x)$

Try these!

Fill in the blanks.

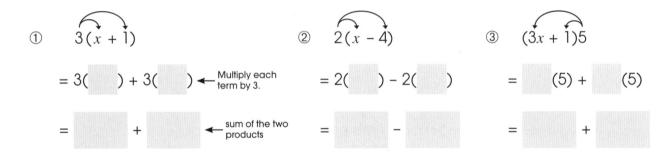

① $3(x + 1)$

$= 3(\quad) + 3(\quad)$ ← Multiply each term by 3.

$= \boxed{\quad} + \boxed{\quad}$ ← sum of the two products

② $2(x - 4)$

$= 2(\quad) - 2(\quad)$

$= \boxed{\quad} - \boxed{\quad}$

③ $(3x + 1)5$

$= \boxed{\quad}(5) + \boxed{\quad}(5)$

$= \boxed{\quad} + \boxed{\quad}$

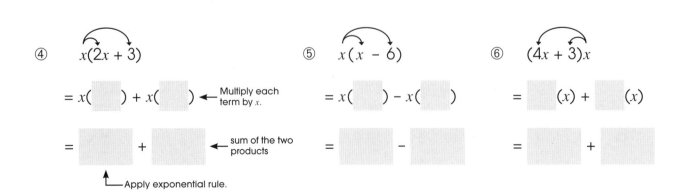

④ $x(2x + 3)$

$= x(\quad) + x(\quad)$ ← Multiply each term by x.

$= \boxed{\quad} + \boxed{\quad}$ ← sum of the two products

└─ Apply exponential rule.

⑤ $x(x - 6)$

$= x(\quad) - x(\quad)$

$= \boxed{\quad} - \boxed{\quad}$

⑥ $(4x + 3)x$

$= \boxed{\quad}(x) + \boxed{\quad}(x)$

$= \boxed{\quad} + \boxed{\quad}$

Expand. Show your work.

⑦　$5(x - 2)$

⑧　$2(6x + 1)$

Hint

A negative sign that goes in front of a bracket represents -1.

$-(a + b) = -a - b$

$-(a - b) = -a + b$

⑨　$(x - 4)2$

⑩　$-3(x - 1)$

⑪　$x(2x + 5)$

⑫　$x(x - 7)$

⑬　$3x(x + 1)$

⑭　$-x(x + 10)$

⑮　$2x(x + 5)$

⑯　$x^2(-x + 5)$

⑰　$(3x + 1)2x$

⑱　$(2x - 3)x^2$

⑲　$2x(4x - 2)$

⑳　$-3x(4x + 1)$

㉑　$2x(x^3 + 3x - 4)$

㉒　$(x^2 - 2x - 3)3x$

㉓ $4x(x + 1 + x^2)$

㉔ $-5x(6 - x^3 + 2x)$

Hint

Remember to arrange the terms in your answers from the one with the highest degree to the one with the lowest.

㉕ $-x^2(x + 4 - x^2)$

㉖ $2x^2(-x^2 + 1 - 2x)$

㉗ $(3x^2 - 4 + x)3x^2$

㉘ $-4x^2(1 - x + 3x^2)$

㉙ $2x^3(2x - 1 + x^2)$

㉚ $(-3x + 5 - x^2)3x^3$

Fill in the missing terms.

Hint

Find the factor using the product of one of the terms. Then check whether you found the correct factor by multiplying it by another term.

e.g. ? $(x^2 + 2x) = 3x^2 + 6x$

? $\times x^2 = 3x^2$

So, ? is 3.

Since $3(2x) = 6x$ is also true, the missing factor must be 3.

㉛ a. ⬜ $(2x^2 + 3x) = 8x^2 + 12x$

b. ⬜ $(x + 4) = 2x^2 + 8x$

c. ⬜ $(3x^2 - x + 1) = -3x^3 + x^2 - x$

d. ⬜ $(6x^3 + x^2 - 2) = 12x^5 + 2x^4 - 4x^2$

㉜ a. $x($ ⬜ $+$ ⬜ $) = 3x^2 + 4x$

b. $2x($ ⬜ $-$ ⬜ $) = 4x^2 - 12x$

c. $x^2($ ⬜ $-$ ⬜ $+$ ⬜ $) = 3x^4 - x^3 + 3x^2$

d. $-3x^2($ ⬜ $-$ ⬜ $-$ ⬜ $) = 6x^4 + 9x^3 + 15x^2$

Expand and evaluate.

㉝ $3x(2x^2 + x)$ $x = -1$ ㉞ $2a(-a - 4)$ $a = 5$

㉟ $-n(6n^2 + n)$ $n = 3$ ㊱ $(m^2 - 8m + 1)3m$ $m = -2$

㊲ $(-k^2 - k + 3)(-6k)$ $k = -3$ ㊳ $(-2u^3 + 3u + 4)(-2u^2)$ $u = 2$

For each rectangle, find the polynomials that represent its perimeter and area. Then evaluate using the given value.

㊴
$x + 3$

x

a. Perimeter:

2(_____ + _____) = _____

Area:

(_____) (_____) = _____

b. Evaluate for $x = 6$.

Perimeter: _____ = _____

Area: _____ = _____

㊵
$x + 4$

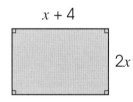

$2x$

a. Perimeter:

_____

Area:

_____

b. Evaluate for $x = 5$.

Perimeter: _____

Area: _____

Solve the problems. Show your work.

㊶ Iris decided to fence her vegetable garden. Its width
   is 2 m shorter than its length.

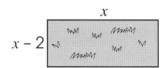

a. Write a polynomial that represents
   how much fencing she needs.

b. How much fencing does she need
   if the length is 5 m?

㊷ George wants to install tiles for the backsplash in his
   bathroom. The length of each tile is 8 cm longer than
   the width.

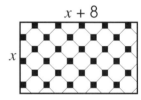

a. Write a polynomial that represents
   the area of each tile.

b. Write a polynomial that represents
   the area of the backsplash if
   20 tiles completely cover it.

㊸ A hexagonal pencil holder is made up of 6 rectangular
   wood panels. The length of each wood panel is 1 cm more
   than 3 times its width.

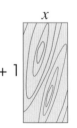

a. Write a polynomial that represents
   the area of all 6 panels.

b. Find how much wood was used if
   the width of each panel is 4 cm.

Answer the questions.

㊹ Expand.

a. $5(x - 1)$ b. $-3(4y + 6)$

c. $p(7p + 3)$ d. $-b(b + 10)$

e. $3n(n + 8)$ f. $-6t(2t - 1)$

g. $2a^2(10a - 3)$ h. $-s^2(s^3 - 2s + 1)$

i. $m^3(m^2 - 5m + 2)$ j. $-8u(-2u^2 + 3u^3 - 1)$

k. $4g^2(9 - g^3 + 3g^2)$ l. $-3v(10v - 5v^3 + v^2)$

m. $x^2(-2 + 3x^2 - y)$ n. $-ab(b^2 + 3a^4 - 2ab)$

> **Note**
>
> **Distributive Property**
>
> $a(b + c) = ab + ac$
>
> $-(a + b) = -a - b$
>
> $-(a - b) = -a + b$
>
> Arrange the terms in a polynomial from the one with the highest degree to the one with the lowest.

㊺ Expand and evaluate for $x = 3$ and $y = -2$.

a. $x(2x + 3)$ b. $2x(x - 5)$

c. $-5y(2y + 1)$ d. $-x(x^2 - 2x + 1)$

e. $3y^2(y^2 - 4y + 5)$ f. $4x^2(-x^2 + 3x - 4)$

㊻ Consider the quadrilaterals below.

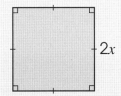
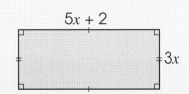
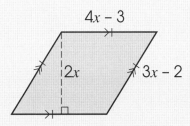

a. Write two polynomials to represent the perimeter and area of each shape.

b. Evaluate the perimeter and area of the parallelogram if $x = 3$ cm.

c. Can the value of x be smaller than 1 cm? Explain.

㊼ A pottery class is having a promotion: the more attendees there are in a group, the lower the cost is for x attendees at $\$(30 - x)$/attendee.

a. Write a polynomial for the total cost for x attendees.

b. What is the total cost if there are 10 attendees?

c. The owner wants to set a limit to the number of attendees. Should the owner set it to 15 people or 20 people to maximize profit? Explain.

Chapter 4

4.4 Operations with Polynomials

Key Ideas

Apply the order of operations to determine which operation to perform first. Keep the key steps below in mind when performing operations with polynomials.

❶ Expand any products of polynomials to remove brackets.

❷ Group the like terms. Be sure to include their "+" or "–" signs.

❸ Add and subtract to simplify.

Write the polynomial in standard form by putting the terms in order from the one with the highest degree to the one with the lowest degree.

Examples

$$3(x - 2) + 5(x + 1)$$

$$= 3(x) - 3(2) + 5(x) + 5(1) \quad \leftarrow \text{Expand each product.}$$

$$= 3x - 6 + 5x + 5$$

$$= 3x + 5x - 6 + 5 \quad \leftarrow \text{Group like terms.}$$

$$= 8x - 1 \quad \leftarrow \text{Add and subtract to simplify.}$$

$$3x(x^2 + 2) - x(x - 3)$$

$$= 3x(x^2) + 3x(2) - x(x) + x(3) \quad \leftarrow \begin{array}{l}\text{Recall:} \\ -(a - b) = -a + b\end{array}$$

$$= 3x^3 + 6x - x^2 + 3x \quad \leftarrow \text{Apply exponential rules.}$$

$$= 3x^3 - x^2 + 6x + 3x \quad \leftarrow \begin{array}{l}\text{Group like terms while} \\ \text{putting them in order.}\end{array}$$

$$= 3x^3 - x^2 + 9x \quad \leftarrow \text{Simplify.}$$

Try these!

Fill in the blanks.

① $3(x - 1) + 2(x - 2)$

$$= \boxed{}\, x - \boxed{}\, (1) + \boxed{}\, x - \boxed{}\, (2)$$

$$= \boxed{}\, x + \boxed{}\, x - \boxed{} - \boxed{}$$

$$= \boxed{}\, x - \boxed{}$$

② $4(2x + 1) - 3(x + 5)$

$$= 4(\boxed{}) + 4(\boxed{}) - 3(\boxed{}) - 3(\boxed{})$$

$$= \boxed{}\, x - \boxed{}\, x + \boxed{} - \boxed{}$$

$$= \boxed{}\, x - \boxed{}$$

③ $x(2x + 3) + 2x(x - 3)$

$$= \boxed{}\, (2x) + \boxed{}\, (3) + \boxed{}\, (x) - \boxed{}\, (3)$$

$$= \boxed{}\, x^2 + \boxed{}\, x^2 + \boxed{}\, x - \boxed{}\, x$$

$$= \boxed{}\, x^2 - \boxed{}\, x$$

④ $5(x^2 + x) - 2x(x - 1)$

$$= 5(\boxed{}) + 5(\boxed{}) - 2x(\boxed{}) + 2x(\boxed{})$$

$$= \boxed{}\, x^2 - \boxed{}\, x^2 + \boxed{}\, x + \boxed{}\, x$$

$$= \boxed{}\, x^2 + \boxed{}\, x$$

Simplify the polynomial expressions. Show your work.

⑤ $4(x + 5) + 6(2x - 1)$

⑥ $8(2x + 7) - x(x + 5)$

⑦ $3x(x - 1) + 2x(3x + 1)$

⑧ $-5x(2x - 3) + 6x(x + 8)$

⑨ $x^2(x - 6) + 2(5x + 4)$

⑩ $4(x^2 + 3x) - x^2(7x + 2)$

⑪ $2x^2(3 + x) - x(x^2 + 4x)$

⑫ $3x(6x^2 - x) - x^3(2x - 3)$

⑬ $-x^2(3x + 1) - 4x(x - 6)$

⑭ $-6x^2(2x - 1) + 7x(x^2 - 1)$

⑮ $7x^2(-x + 6) - x(x^2 + 5x)$

⑯ $-4x^2(-2x + 1) - 3x(-2x^2 - 1)$

Simplify. Then evaluate with the given values.

⑰ $3(x + 2) - 5(2x - 1)$ $x = 3$

⑱ $4x(3x - 1) + 6(x + 1)$ $x = 1$

⑲ $2x(x - 1) + 3x(x + 2)$ $x = -1$

⑳ $x(3x + 2) - 2x(x + 5)$ $x = -2$

㉑ $2x^2(x + 5) + x^2(3x - 1)$ $x = 5$

㉒ $-x^2(2x + 4) + x^2(4x - 3)$ $x = -3$

㉓ $\frac{1}{2}x(6x + 2) + \frac{1}{3}(9x + 15)$ $x = 2$

㉔ $\frac{2}{3}x(9x + 6) - \frac{1}{4}(8x - 12)$ $x = -1$

Circle the correct polynomial that represents each scenario and simplify it. Then evaluate.

㉕ An indoor playground charges an entrance fee of $6 plus $2/h for adults and a fee of $3 plus $1/h for children. What was the total cost for a party of 5 adults and 10 children who spent h hours at the playground?

    A. $C = 5(6h + 2) + 10(3h - 1)$

    B. $C = 5(6 + 2h) + 10(3 + h)$

Find the total cost if the group spent 3 hours at the playground.

㉖ A lemonade booth has a start-up cost of $500 and a running cost of $200/day. A game booth has a start-up cost of $1200 and a running cost of $150/day. What is the total cost of running 2 lemonade booths and 3 game booths for d days?

    A. $C = 2(500 + 200d) + 3(1200 + 150d)$

    B. $C = d(500 + 2d) + d(1200 + 3d)$

Find the total cost of running the booths for 2 weeks.

㉗ Installing a bowling lane costs $2000 and earns $400/month. A mini-golf station costs $800 to build and earns $250/month. How much more profit is gained from 6 bowling lanes than 9 mini-golf stations after m months in operation?

    A. $P = 6(400m - 2000) - 9(250m - 800)$

    B. $P = 6(2000 + 400m) - 9(800 + 250m)$

Find the difference in profit after 35 months.

Answer the questions. Show your work.

㉘ Lisa is considering two portfolios of a mix of stocks for investing.

Stock	Present Value	Predicted Growth
A	$220	$3/year
B	$180	$4/year
C	$140	$7/year

- Portfolio A:

  3 shares of Stock A

  5 shares of Stock B

  5 shares of Stock C

- Portfolio B:

  4 shares of Stock A

  3 shares of Stock B

  6 shares of Stock C

a. Determine a simplified expression that represents the value of each portfolio after y years.

b. Use the expressions to determine the value of each portfolio after 5 years.

㉙ A picture frame has the dimensions as shown.

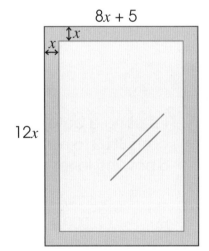

a. Determine the simplified expressions that represent the outer perimeter and the area of the frame.

b. Use the expressions to determine the outer perimeter and the area of the frame if $x = 6$ cm.

Answer the questions.

㉚ Simplify the polynomials.

a. $5(x + 6) + 2(-x - 8)$

b. $2x(x - 4) - 3x(x - 6)$

c. $-6x(x + 1) + 5x(3x + 1)$

d. $x^2(2x + 3) - 4(5x - 4)$

e. $-2x^2(2x - 1) + x^2(3x + 5)$

f. $5x(x^2 - 1) + x^2(2x + 3)$

g. $9(x^2 - 3x + 2) + 3x^2(x + 1)$

> **Note**
>
> **To simplify polynomials:**
>
> ❶ Expand any products of polynomials to remove brackets.
>
> ❷ Group the like terms with their "+" or "–" signs.
>
> ❸ Add and subtract to simplify.

㉛ Simplify and evaluate each expression for $a = 2$ and $b = -1$.

a. $8(6a + 2) - 7a$

b. $7b(b + 4) - 6b^2$

c. $-4a(1 - a) + a$

d. $6 - b(5b + 3)$

e. $2a(-3a - 2) + a(a^2 - 1)$

f. $b^2(2b + 7) + 3b(b - 1)$

㉜ Explain the benefit of simplifying a polynomial expression before evaluating it by substitution.

㉝ The production of a book includes a base cost of $500 plus a printing cost of $2.30/copy in colour and $1.75/copy in black and white.

a. Write an expression to represent the total cost of producing the same number of copies, c, of a book in colour and in black and white.

b. How much does it cost to produce and print a book of 2000 copies in colour and in black and white?

㉞ On average, a household consumes 5 kWh of electricity during on-peak hours and 18 kWh during off-peak hours on a weekday, and 2 kWh of electricity during on-peak hours and 10 kWh during off-peak hours on a weekend.

a. Write an expression to show the household's cost of electricity of one week at $x/kWh during on-peak hours and $y/kWh during off-peak hours.

b. Use the expression to find the cost of electricity of one week if the rate is $0.13/kWh for on-peak hours and $0.06/kWh for off-peak hours.

Things I have learned in this chapter:

• identifying monomials, binomials, and trinomials

• determining the degree of a term and a polynomial

• grouping like terms

• adding and subtracting polynomials

• multiplying polynomials with monomials

• representing word problems with polynomials

My Notes:

_____

_____

_____

_____

_____

_____

_____

_____

_____

_____

Chapter 4

Knowledge and Understanding

Circle the correct answers.

① Which of the following is not a monomial?

   A. $4x$

   B. 0

   C. xy^2

   D. $x - 1$

② Which term in $-2x^2y + 2xy - y^2$ has a coefficient of 2?

   A. $-2x^2y$

   B. $2xy$

   C. $-y^2$

   D. none of the above

③ Which term in $4x^2y^2 - 3x^3y + 5xy^2$ has a degree of 3?

   A. $4x^2y^2$

   B. $-3x^3y$

   C. $5xy^2$

   D. none of the above

④ Which is a binomial with a degree of 2?

   A. $2x + 5$

   B. $4x^2$

   C. $4x^2 + 5x$

   D. $x^2 + 3x - 1$

⑤ Which of the following is not a like term of the others?

   A. $5xy^2$

   B. $-5xy^2$

   C. $-3x^2y$

   D. $3xy^2$

⑥ What is the degree of the polynomial $2xy^3 + 3xy - 4y^2$?

   A. 1

   B. 2

   C. 3

   D. 4

⑦ What is the product of a non-zero monomial and a trinomial?

   A. a monomial

   B. a binomial

   C. a trinomial

   D. not sufficient information

Rewrite each polynomial in standard form. Then write the degree of the polynomial.

⑧   **Standard Form**   **Degree**

a. $2x + x^2$ _____   _____

b. $4y - 3 + 6y^2$ _____   _____

c. $-3a - a^3 + 7$ _____   _____

d. $8x^3 - 4 + 6x - 7x^2$ _____   _____

e. $12 + 6c^2 - 10c^3d + 8cd$ _____   _____

f. $5i^3 - ij + 2i^2j - 3i^2j^2$ _____   _____

Simplify the polynomials. Show your work.

⑨ $(3a + 1) + (2a - 2)$ ⑩ $(3x + 4) - (2x + 2)$

⑪ $(x^2 + 3x - 4) + (2x^2 - 4x)$ ⑫ $(2y^2 - 10) - (3y^2 + 4y)$

⑬ $6x(2x + 1)$ ⑭ $2a(a - 5)$

⑮ $-3y(-y + 2)$

⑯ $(x^2 - 3x + 1)2x$

⑰ $4(3x - 1) + 2(2x + 5)$

⑱ $0.4(2x + 10) + x(6x + 2)$

⑲ $2a(a^2 + 2a - 1) + a^2(a - 1)$

⑳ $\dfrac{1}{2}n(4n + 2) - \dfrac{2}{3}n^2(9n - 6)$

Determine the missing monomial in each product. Then evaluate each expression for $x = -1$. Show your work.

㉑   ▯ $(3x + 2) = 15x + 10$

㉒   ▯ $(x^2 - 4x + 3) = 2x^3 - 8x^2 + 6x$

㉓   ▯ $(-2x^2 + 3x - 1) = 16x^3 - 24x^2 + 8x$

㉔   ▯ $(-x^2 - 2x + 4) = -4x^4 - 8x^3 + 16x^2$

㉕   ▯ $(3x^2 - 2x + 10) = -15x^3 + 10x^2 - 50x$

㉖   ▯ $(-2x - 12) = 12x^3 + 72x^2$

Application

Solve the problems. Show your work.

㉗ Write expressions to represent the perimeter and the area of each shape.

Shape	Perimeter	Area
$3xy$ (square)		
$6x - 7$, $2x$ (rectangle)		
$5x - 3$, $4x$, $3x + 6$ (parallelogram)		
$x + 3$, $2x + 3$, $2x$, $3x - 1$ (trapezoid)		

㉘ A spa charges $50 plus $10/half hour for a massage and $35 plus $8/half hour for a facial.

a. Write an expression that represents the total cost for t half hours of both services.

b. What is the total cost if a client received both services for 1.5 hours?

㉙ The cost of a medication for a patient is $12/dose plus a dispensing fee of $21.

    a. Write an expression that represents the cost of the medication for 4 patients if they all require d doses for a treatment.

    b. Find the total medication cost of the 4 patients if 12 doses are needed.

㉚ Belmont High School received four donations of $6000 each for math scholarships and nine donations of $3000 each for science scholarships this year. Every year, each math scholarship awards $300 and each science scholarship awards $500 to top students.

    a. Write an expression that represents the remaining donations after y years of awarding the top students.

    b. Find the remaining donations after 4 years of awarding the top students.

Communication

Answer the questions.

㉛ Describe how the degree of a polynomial is determined.

㉜ Leo says, "A monomial can contain any number of variables, including having none at all." Is he correct? Explain.

㉝ Joanne added 3 different terms and simplified the sum into a monomial. Explain how this is possible. Give an example.

Thinking

Find the answers.

㉞ Find the missing polynomials.

a. [   ] $(4x^2 - 2x + 10) = 2x^2y - xy + 5y$

b. $2a($ [   ] $) = 4a^3 - 18a^2 + 0.2a$

c. $4(3x + 1) + 2x($ [   ] $) = 6x^2 + 2x + 4$

㉟ Expand and simplify.

a. $(x + 3)(2x + 1)$ b. $(y + 1)(3y - 2)$

㊱ There is a total of 25 quarters and dimes in a piggy bank. Write an expression to represent the total value of the coins. Then find the number of each coin there are if the total value is $5.05.

Final Test

Circle the correct answers.

① Which of the following is not a rational number?

    A. 105%
                          B. $\dfrac{25}{11}$

    C. $\sqrt{2}$
                            D. -0.09

② Which power is equivalent to 3^{-2}?

    A. $(-3)^2$
                         B. $-\dfrac{1}{3^2}$

    C. -3^2
                           D. $\dfrac{1}{3^2}$

③ Which of the following is not expressed in scientific notation?

    A. -1.2×10^1
                   B. 1×10^{-8}

    C. 0.5×10^6
                   D. 2.3×10^4

④ Which of the following can be simplified to x^2?

    A. $(x^{-1})^{-2}$
                   B. $x^3 - x$

    C. $\sqrt{x^2}$
                     D. $\dfrac{x^3}{x^{-1}}$

⑤ Which polynomial is a monomial?

    A. $3xy$
                            B. $3x + 10$

    C. $2(x^2 + 1)$
                   D. $x^2 + 2x - 2$

⑥ Which polynomial has a degree of 2?

    A. $2x - y$
                          B. $4(x + 1)$

    C. $-x^2$
                          D. $x^3 + 3xy$

⑦ How many terms will there be when $3(x + 1) - 2x(x - 3)$ is simplified?

    A. 1
                               B. 2

    C. 3
                               D. 4

Evaluate. Show your work.

⑧ $5\sqrt{10} \div \sqrt{2}$

⑨ $(3\sqrt{2})^2$

⑩ $(3.5 \times 10^2) \div (7 \times 10^{-1})$

⑪ $3^{-1} \times 3^3 \div 3^2$

⑫ $(-7)^4 \times (7^2)^3$

⑬ $10^2 \div (10^{-1})^{-2} \times \dfrac{1}{10^3}$

Simplify the expressions. Show your work.

⑭ $\dfrac{x^3 y^2}{xy^3}$

⑮ $(ab)^2 (a^{-1})$

⑯ $\left(\dfrac{4x^3 y^2}{2x^2}\right)\left(\dfrac{3xy^2}{y}\right)$

⑰ $(n + n)(n^2)^{-3}$

⑱ $-i^2 (3i^2 - i^2)$

⑲ $\sqrt{4a^2} \left(\dfrac{a}{3}\right)$

Simplify the polynomials and evaluate them with the given values. Show your work.

⑳ Simplify and evaluate for $x = 2$.

    a. $(6x + 4) + (5x - 2)$

    b. $4(x + 1) - (-2x)$

㉑ Simplify and evaluate for $y = -3$.

    a. $5(y - 4) + 2(y - 2)$

    b. $2y(y + 5) - 3y(-y - 1)$

Solve for x. Show your work.

㉒ $\dfrac{4}{7}x + 2 = 14$

㉓ $8(x - 6) = -56$

㉔ $\dfrac{x}{8} = \dfrac{7}{2}$

㉕ $\dfrac{3x + 1}{4} = \dfrac{1}{2}$

㉖ $10 - 3\sqrt{x} = 7$

㉗ $4x + 5 = 2x - 11$

Write "T" for the true statements and "F" for the false ones.

㉘ All terminating and repeating decimals are rational numbers. _____

㉙ The sum of a negative number and a positive number is always positive. _____

㉚ A rate is a comparison of two quantities with the same unit of measure. _____

㉛ The square root of a negative number cannot be evaluated. _____

㉜ In scientific notation, a positive exponent in the power of 10 implies that the number is positive. _____

㉝ A monomial subtracted from a binomial can result in a trinomial. _____

Application

Solve the problems. Show your work.

㉞ A mobile application had a revenue of $\$8.164 \times 10^6$ last year. What was its weekly revenue? Write your answer in scientific notation.

③⑤ A cookie recipe specifies a ratio of milk to flour to be 2:5. For more servings, Jane needed 5 cups of milk for the dough. If she already added 8 cups of flour to the milk, how many more cups of flour does she need to add? Set up an equation to solve.

③⑥ A triangular tile has an area of $3\sqrt{15}$ cm². If its base measures $2\sqrt{5}$ cm, what is its height? Give an exact answer.

③⑦ There are 25 quarters and some dimes that are worth a total of $8.35 in a piggy bank. How many dimes are there? Set up an equation to solve.

③⑧ Mrs. Joe added $\frac{5}{6}$ of a ladle of olive oil to 50 mL of coconut oil to make a 175-mL solution. What is the capacity of the ladle? Set up an equation to solve.

③⑨ Each month, Ben earns $600 and donates $20 to each charity, while Steve earns $850 and donates $25 to each charity. They both donate to x charities each month.

a. Write a simplified expression to represent their total savings in m months.

b. How much will they save after 6 months if they donate to 3 charities?

Answer the questions.

㊽ Explain why $\sqrt{64}$ is a rational number and $\sqrt{23}$ is not.

㊶ Judy says, "For powers with the same positive integer as their bases, the one with the greater exponent is greater." Is she correct? Explain.

㊷ List three laws of exponents. Give an example for each with numerical values.

㊸ Explain how the sum of two trinomials results in a binomial. Give an example.

Thinking

Find the answers.

㊹ Solve for x.

a. $\dfrac{\sqrt{8x}}{2} = \dfrac{4}{\sqrt{2x}}$

b. $3\sqrt{7} = \sqrt{x^3 - 1}$

㊺ Find the missing polynomials.

a. $\left(\ ?\ \right)(3x - 2y + 2) = 6xy - 4y^2 + 4y$

b. $-2a\left(\ ?\ \right) = 4a^2 + 2ab - 6a$

㊻ Find the specified measurements of the cube and the square in terms of x.

a. 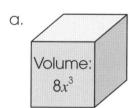 Surface Area:

Volume:
$8x^3$

b. Perimeter:

Area:
$20x^4$

㊼ There are 430 coins with twice as many quarters as dimes and the rest being nickels. They are worth a total of $53. How many of each coin are there? Set up an equation to solve.

Chapter 1: Numeracy

1.1 Integers

1. 3
2. -4
3. -3
4. 0

5. − ; 3   6. − ; 7   7. + ; 9

8. = -9 − 5   9. = 2 − 8   10. = -4 − 5
   = -14   = -6   = -9

11. = -3 + 1   12. = -5 + 8   13. = -7 − 10
    = -2   = 3   = -17

14. +   15. +   16. −   17. +
18. +   19. +   20. −   21. −
22. -9   23. 30   24. -3   25. -15
26. 42   27. -27   28. 8   29. -7
30. 35   31. -7   32. -8   33. 15
34. 20 ; 18

35. = (+5) − (-5)
    = 10

36. = (-4) − (-8)   37. = (-4) ÷ (-4)
    = 4   = 1

38. = (-10) + 9 x 2   39. = (5 − 9) ÷ (-2)
    = (-10) + 18   = (-4) ÷ (-2)
    = 8   = 2

40. = $(3)^2$ − 4   41. = 1 + $(2)^2$ − 12
    = 9 − 4   = 1 + 4 − 12
    = 5   = -7

42. = ((-1) x 16) − (-16) 43. = $((6+5) − 7)^2$
    = (-16) + 16   = $(11 − 7)^2$
    = 0   = 4^2
                               = 16

44. = (4 − 5) x ((-4) − 7)
    = (-1) x (-11)
    = 11

45. = ((-1) + 9) ÷ ((-2) + 4)
    = 8 ÷ 2
    = 4

46. = $((-1) + 2)^2$ x $(-3)^2$
    = 1^2 x $(-3)^2$
    = 1 x 9
    = 9

47. = $((-4) + 9)^2$ ÷ (4 − 9)
    = 5^2 ÷ (-5)
    = 25 ÷ (-5)
    = -5

48a. 2   b. 6   c. 0   d. -16
  e. 2   f. -20   g. 4   h. 45

49a. -12   b. -22   c. 17   d. -34
  e. -41   f. 19   g. -2   h. 40
50a. -35   b. -42   c. -13   d. 3
  e. -147   f. 2   g. 85   h. 5

51. (Suggested answer)
    2.5 and 70% are examples of a decimal and a percent that are not integers.

52. The expression will yield a positive number because the last operation is squaring the value (an exponent of 2), which always results in a positive number.

53. $(8 x (-4))^2$ is the greater expression because it has a positive answer while 8^2 x (-4) has a negative answer.

54. The unknown is a negative integer.

55. The net profit was -$20.

56. The average daily temperature was -1°C.

1.2 Rational Numbers and Irrational Numbers

1. R ; 3   2. R ; -8 ; 1
3. I   4. R ; 0 ; any number other than 0
5. R ; 7 ; 10   6. R ; 21 ; 100
7. I   8. R ; 4 ; 3
9. R ; -19 ; 10   10. R ; -5 ; 4
11. I   12. R ; -1 ; 100

13. (Circle all except g and j.)
    (Suggested answers for fractions)
    a. $\frac{5}{1}$ b. $\frac{8}{5}$ c. $-\frac{8}{10}$ d. $\frac{3}{1}$
    e. $-\frac{5}{2}$ f. $-\frac{9}{1}$ h. $\frac{115}{100}$ i. $\frac{301}{100}$
    k. $\frac{9}{1}$ l. $-\frac{1009}{1000}$ m. $\frac{4}{1}$ n. $-\frac{4}{2}$
    o. $\frac{22}{20}$ p. $\frac{0}{1}$

14a. $-2\frac{1}{2}$, -9, -1.009, $-\frac{4}{\sqrt{4}}$ b. 5, 3.01, $(-3)^2$, 2^2

  c. $1\frac{3}{5}$, -0.8, 1.15, $\frac{2.2}{2}$, $\frac{0}{1^2}$

15. = $\frac{4}{12}$ + $\frac{3}{12}$ 16. = $\frac{8}{10}$ − $\frac{5}{10}$
    = $\frac{7}{12}$ = $\frac{3}{10}$

17. = $-\frac{8}{12}$ + $1\frac{9}{12}$ 18. = $\frac{6}{30}$ − $\frac{25}{30}$
    = $1\frac{1}{12}$ = $-\frac{19}{30}$

19. = $\frac{6}{8}$ − $\frac{1}{8}$ 20. = $\frac{14}{20}$ − $\frac{15}{20}$
    = $-\frac{7}{8}$ = $-\frac{1}{20}$

21. = 2.3 + 1.2   22. = 4.5 − 2.4
    = 3.5   = 2.1
    = $3\frac{1}{2}$ = $2\frac{1}{10}$

Answers

23. $= \frac{10}{60} - \frac{42}{60}$

$= -\frac{32}{60}$

$= -\frac{8}{15}$

24. $= 2.05 - 0.45$

$= 1.6$

$= 1\frac{3}{5}$

25. $= \frac{1}{12}$

26. $= -\frac{2}{15}$

27. $= \frac{5}{8} \times -\frac{3}{5}$

$= -\frac{3}{8}$

28. $= -\frac{14}{5} \times \frac{10}{7}$

$= -4$

29. $= 9 \times \frac{3}{1}$

$= 27$

30. $= 10 \times \frac{4}{3}$

$= 13\frac{1}{3}$

31. $= -\frac{15}{4} \times \frac{4}{1}$

$= -15$

32. $= \frac{7}{8} \times -\frac{2}{1}$

$= -1\frac{3}{4}$

33. $= \frac{3}{2} \times \frac{5}{2}$

$= 3\frac{3}{4}$

34. $= -\frac{9}{4} \times 100$

$= -225$

35. $= \frac{5}{2} \times \frac{4}{5}$

$= 2$

36. $= -\frac{16}{5} \times -\frac{9}{8}$

$= 3\frac{3}{5}$

37. $= -\frac{5}{9} + \frac{3}{9}$

$= -\frac{2}{9}$

38. $= -3 - \frac{14}{5} \times \frac{10}{7}$

$= -3 - 4$

$= -7$

39. $= 14 \div (\frac{2}{4} + \frac{5}{4})$

$= 14 \div \frac{7}{4}$

$= 14 \times \frac{4}{7}$

$= 8$

40. $= -\frac{1}{3} + \frac{16}{9} \times -\frac{3}{4}$

$= -\frac{1}{3} - \frac{4}{3}$

$= -\frac{5}{3}$

41. $= \frac{2}{5} \times -\frac{5}{6} + \frac{1}{3}$

$= -\frac{1}{3} + \frac{1}{3}$

$= 0$

42. $= -\frac{9}{7} \times \frac{8}{3} + \frac{4}{7}$

$= -\frac{24}{7} + \frac{4}{7}$

$= -2\frac{6}{7}$

43. $= -\frac{15}{8} \times \frac{6}{5} + \frac{1}{4}$

$= -\frac{9}{4} + \frac{1}{4}$

$= -2$

44. $= -\frac{6}{7} \times -\frac{14}{8} + \frac{1}{2}$

$= \frac{3}{2} + \frac{1}{2}$

$= 2$

45. $= (\frac{2}{4} - \frac{3}{4}) \times (\frac{15}{4} \times -\frac{8}{9})$

$= -\frac{1}{4} \times -\frac{10}{3}$

$= \frac{5}{6}$

46a. Set A: $\frac{1}{7}$, $\frac{0}{9}$, $-\frac{3}{4}$, $\frac{\sqrt{9}}{3}$, $-\frac{14}{8}$, $1\frac{5}{9}$

Set B: -9, 0.35, -2.5, 5.2, 0, $-\sqrt{4}$

Set C: 0.55, $-\frac{2}{9}$, $\frac{4}{15}$, -5.11, 2.08, $\frac{13}{7}$

b. Set A: $-\frac{14}{8}$, $-\frac{3}{4}$, $\frac{0}{9}$, $\frac{1}{7}$, $\frac{\sqrt{9}}{3}$, $1\frac{5}{9}$

Set B: -9, -2.5, $-\sqrt{4}$, 0, 0.35, 5.2

Set C: -5.11, $-\frac{2}{9}$, $\frac{4}{15}$, 0.55, $\frac{13}{7}$, 2.08

47a. true ; All integers can be written as a fraction with a denominator of 1.

b. true ; All terminating decimals can be written as fractions with integers as numerators and powers of 10 as denominators.

c. false ; Only square roots of perfect squares are integers and integers are rational.

d. false; Even though $\frac{1}{3}$ is not a terminating decimal, its numerator and denominator are both integers. So it is a rational number.

48. The total cost is $40.50.

49. She practised yoga for $2\frac{7}{8}$ h weekly on average.

50. He made 12 cups of fruit punch.

1.3 Ratio, Rate, and Proportion

1a. 3 ; 3:5 ; 8:3   b. 4 ; 4:7 ; 7:11

2a. 2 ; 3:2 ; 2:5   b. 5 ; 4:5 ; 5:9

3a. 5:6   b. 1:1   c. 11:12

4. 6   5. 12   6. 4   7. 1   8. 18

9. 3   10. 1   11. 2   12. 9   13. 8

14. 6   a. 24 cookies ; 48 cookies

   b. 4 packages ; 2 packages

15. 20 km/h   a. 40 km ; 100 km ; 160 km

   b. 3 h ; 1 h ; 1.5 h

16. $24/shirt   a. $48 ; $144 ; $312

   b. 4 shirts ; 3 shirts ; 9 shirts

17. $4x = 3 \times 16$

$x = 12$

18. $2x = 5 \times 10$

$x = 25$

19. $2x = 8 \times 3$

$x = 12$

20. $21x = 7 \times 33$

$x = 11$

21. $10x = 7 \times 7$

$x = 4.9$

22. $4x = 5 \times 10$

$x = 12.5$

23. $25x = 3 \times 12$

$x = 1.44$

24. $10x = 18 \times 3$

$x = 5.4$

25. $5x = 4 \times 21$

$x = 16.8$

26. $6x = 1.2 \times 5$

$x = 1$

27. 60

$5x = 3 \times 100$

$x = 60$

28. 25

$\frac{1}{4} = \frac{x}{100}$

$4x = 1 \times 100$

$x = 25$

29. 58

$\frac{29}{50} = \frac{x}{100}$

$50x = 29 \times 100$

$x = 58$

30. 13

$\frac{26}{100} = \frac{x}{50}$

$100x = 26 \times 50$

$x = 13$

31. 9

$$\frac{45}{100} = \frac{x}{20}$$
$$100x = 45 \times 20$$
$$x = 9$$

32a. There are 18 red balls.
  b. There are 60 green balls.
  c. There are 21 red balls and 28 green balls.
  d. No, it is not possible to have a total of 60 red and green balls because the total number of balls must be divisible by 7.

33. Jeff reads faster.

34. He needs to type 250 words more.

35a. 6 cups of pancake mix, 4 eggs, and 1 cup of milk are needed for 10 servings.

  b. $7\frac{1}{5}$ cups of pancake mix, $4\frac{4}{5}$ eggs, and $1\frac{1}{5}$ cups of milk are needed for 12 servings.

36a. She answered 17 questions correctly on the English quiz.
  b. There were 60 questions on the Math quiz.
  c. She would have a better score on the English quiz.

37. 60% of the downstairs project will remain when the upstairs project is completed.

20. $= -\frac{7}{20} \times \frac{5}{14}$
    $= -\frac{1}{4} \times \frac{1}{2}$
    $= -\frac{1}{8}$

21. $= -\frac{17}{5} \div \frac{1}{5}$
    $= -\frac{17}{5} \times \frac{5}{1}$
    $= -17$

22. $= \frac{9}{2} \times -\frac{4}{9}$
    $= \frac{1}{1} \times -\frac{2}{1}$
    $= -2$

23. $= -\frac{13}{10} \times \frac{3}{2} \times \frac{5}{1}$
    $= -\frac{13}{2} \times \frac{3}{2} \times 1$
    $= -9\frac{3}{4}$

24. $= \frac{3}{4} \times \frac{2}{5} - \frac{3}{2}$
    $= \frac{3}{2} \times \frac{1}{5} - \frac{3}{2}$
    $= \frac{3}{10} - \frac{3}{2}$
    $= -1\frac{1}{5}$

25. $= 16 - (-\frac{4}{5} \times \frac{5}{10})$
    $= 16 + \frac{2}{5}$
    $= 16\frac{2}{5}$

26. $= (\frac{2}{4} - \frac{3}{4}) \times 5.5$
    $= -\frac{1}{4} \times \frac{11}{2}$
    $= -1\frac{3}{8}$

27. $= -\frac{13}{10} \times \frac{5}{2} \times \frac{4}{1}$
    $= -13$

28. $= (\frac{16}{10} - \frac{21}{10}) \times 1^2$
    $= -\frac{5}{10}$
    $= -\frac{1}{2}$

Quiz 1

1. D   2. A   3. A   4. C
5. C   6. D   7. A

8. $= 18$

9. $= 16 + 3$
   $= 19$

10. $= 12 - 7$
    $= 5$

11. $= (-4) + (-9)$
    $= -13$

12. $= 2 + 4$
    $= 6$

13. $= 1 \times 9$
    $= 9$

14. $= 25 - 9 \times 4$
    $= 25 - 36$
    $= -11$

15. $= 16 \times (-5) - (-2)$
    $= (-80) + 2$
    $= -78$

16. $= ((-3) + 5) \times 4$
    $= 2 \times 4$
    $= 8$

17. $= \frac{28}{8} - \frac{5}{8}$
    $= \frac{23}{8}$
    $= 2\frac{7}{8}$

18. $= \frac{52}{12} - \frac{3}{12}$
    $= \frac{49}{12}$
    $= 4\frac{1}{12}$

19. $= \frac{5}{9} \times \frac{3}{10}$
    $= \frac{1}{3} \times \frac{1}{2}$
    $= \frac{1}{6}$

29a. 5:3   b. 8:9   c. 19:14
30a. 4:2:1   b. 8:6:5   c. 4:3
31. 8   32. 6   33. 2
34. 16   35. 2.5   36. 4
37. 49   38. 25   39. 5
40. 12 oranges/bag   41. 6 km/h
42. $3/can   43. 4 muffins/box
44. 12.5 m/min   45. $7.25/carton

46. $3x = 5 \times 9$
    $x = 15$

47. $5x = 7 \times 15$
    $x = 21$

48. $4x = 8 \times 15$
    $x = 30$

49. $4x = 10 \times 5$
    $x = 12.5$

50. $12x = 3 \times (-4)$
    $x = -1$

51. $2x = 7 \times (-6)$
    $x = -21$

52. $\frac{5}{6} = \frac{2}{x}$
    $5x = 6 \times 2$
    $x = 2.4$

53. $\frac{x}{5} = \frac{3}{4}$
    $4x = 5 \times 3$
    $x = 3.75$

54. $\frac{3}{x} = \frac{2}{5}$
    $2x = 3 \times 5$
    $x = 7.5$

55. Cost before tax:
    $12.50 \times 3 + $9.25 \times 2 = $56
    Cost Including tax:
    $56 + $56 \times 13% = $63.28
    Change: $70 - $63.28 = $6.72
    Her change was $6.72.

Answers

56. Store A: $19.20 ÷ 6 jars = $3.20/jar
    Store B: $15 ÷ 4 jars = $3.75/jar
    Store A offers a better buy.

57a. $((-3) + (-4) + (-11) + 9 + (-2) + 10 + (-6)) ÷ 7 = -1$
    The daily average temperature was -1°C.

  b. Following Sunday's temperature: $(-6) \times 2 = -12$
    Difference in temperature: $-3 - (-12) = 9$
    The difference in temperature was 9°C.

58. If the length of the park is 30 m, let x be the width:
    $6:4 = 30:x$
    $\dfrac{6}{4} = \dfrac{30}{x}$
    $6x = 4 \times 30$
    $x = 20$
    Area: $30 \times 20 = 600$ (m²)
    If the width of the park is 30 m, let x be the length:
    $6:4 = x:30$
    $\dfrac{6}{4} = \dfrac{x}{30}$
    $4x = 6 \times 30$
    $x = 45$
    Area: $45 \times 30 = 1350$ (m²)
    The possible areas are 600 m² and 1350 m².

59. Alcohol in 2-L solution: $2 \times 80\% = 1.6$
    Water in 2-L solution: $2 - 1.6 = 0.4$
    Let x be the amount of water in the final solution:
    $3:8 = x:1.6$
    $\dfrac{3}{8} = \dfrac{x}{1.6}$
    $8x = 3 \times 1.6$
    $x = 0.6$
    Water to be added: $0.6 - 0.4 = 0.2$
    200 mL of water needs to be added.

60. An addition of -5 and a number greater than 5 will yield a positive answer. So, $a > 5$.
    e.g. $-5 + 6 = 1$
    A subtraction where a number smaller than -5 is subtracted from -5 will yield a positive answer. So, $a < -5$.
    e.g. $(-5) - (-6) = 1$

61. All terminating decimals can be expressed as a fraction with a denominator that is a power of 10 and a numerator that is an integer. Therefore, all terminating decimals are rational numbers.

62. No. The square of any integers, positive or negative, must be greater than (e.g. $(-3)^2 = 9 > 0$) or equal to 0 (i.e. $0^2 = 0$). This is because squaring a number is simply multiplying a number by itself. In multiplication, same signs yield a positive answer. Hence, a squared number cannot be negative.

63a. $\dfrac{0.6}{x} = (-\dfrac{3}{10}) \times (-\dfrac{3}{10})$
    $\dfrac{0.6}{x} = \dfrac{9}{100}$
    $9x = 0.6 \times 100$
    $x = 6\dfrac{2}{3}$

  b. $(-1.2 + x) \times 3 = 9 + 3$
    $(-1.2 + x) \times 3 = 12$
    $(-1.2 + x) = 4$
    $x = 5.2$

64a. $(b - a)^2$ yields a positive answer because the final operation is a square, which always results in a positive value.

  b. $b(a - b)$ yields a negative answer. Since $a > 0$ and $b < 0$, $(a - b)$ is always positive. b is negative, so the product of b and $(a - b)$ always yields a negative answer.

Chapter 2: Exponents

2.1 Exponential Notation

1. 2	2. 3	3. 4	4. 5
5. 6	6. 8	7. 3	8. 7
9. 0	10. 4	11. 0	12. 1
13. 5	14. 7	15. 5	16. 6
17. 2 ; 5	18. 8 ; 8	19. 2^4	20. 4^3
21. 5^3	22. 8^4	23. 7^5	24. 6^6
25. 12^1	26. 3^7	27. 0^4	28. 9^5

29. 4×4 30. $5 \times 5 \times 5$
31. $2 \times 2 \times 2 \times 2$ 32. $3 \times 3 \times 3 \times 3 \times 3$
33. $6 \times 6 \times 6$ 34. $8 \times 8 \times 8 \times 8$
35. $5 \times 5 \times 5 \times 5 \times 5$ 36. $0 \times 0 \times 0 \times 0 \times 0 \times 0$
37. $10 \times 10 \times 10$ 38. 7

39. 9	40. 25	41. 49	42. 1
43. 81	44. 1	45. 64	46. 16

47. 0 48. $3^3 \times 4^2$
49. $2^3 \times 5^2$ 50. $2^3 \times 3^4$
51. $4^3 \times 7^3$ 52. $2^2 \times 3^2 \times 6^2$
53. $4^1 \times 5^3 \times 9^2$ 54. $5^1 \times 6^2 \times 8^3$
55. (-2) ; 4 56. $(-3) \times (-3) \times (-3)$; -27

57. $(-4) \times (-4)$; 16   58. $(-5) \times (-5) \times (-5)$; -125
59. >   60. <   61. <   62. >
63. >   64. <   65. <   66. >
67. <   68. >   69. <   70. >
71. 2 ; 3   72. 2 ; 5 ; 5
    2 ; 3 ; 2^2 ; 3^2 $2 \times 2 \times 5 \times 5$; $2^2 \times 5^2$

73.
```
        4              4
      /   \          /   \
    2      2       2      2
```
$2 \times 2 \times 2 \times 2$; 2^4

74.
```
        6              9
      /   \          /   \
    2      3       3      3
```
$2 \times 3 \times 3 \times 3$; $2^1 \times 3^3$

75a. 9   b. 16   c. 27
d. -25   e. 1000   f. -49
g. -512   h. 81   i. 1
j. 16   k. -125   l. -64
m. 0   n. 1   o. 125
p. $\frac{4}{9}$ q. $\frac{1}{16}$ r. $\frac{1}{125}$
s. $-\frac{1}{27}$ t. $\frac{4}{25}$ u. $-\frac{25}{49}$
v. $-\frac{4}{81}$ w. 1   x. $-\frac{27}{64}$

76. (Suggested answers)
a. 3^2 ; 9^1 b. 5^2 ; $(-5)^2$ c. 7^2 ; $(-7)^2$
d. 2^4 ; 4^2 e. $(-1)^3$; $(-1)^5$ f. 3^4 ; 9^2
g. 0^2 ; 0^4 h. 5^4 ; 25^2 i. -2^2 ; -4^1
j. -8^2 ; $(-4)^3$

77. Yes, he is correct. Every perfect square
can be expressed as a square of its positive
square root and a square of its negative
square root.
e.g. $9 = 3^2$
$9 = (-3)^2$

78a. $2^1 \times 5^3$ b. $2^4 \times 3^2$ c. $2^2 \times 3^4$
d. $2^3 \times 3^1 \times 5^2$ e. $2^1 \times 3^3 \times 5^2$

79. $(-2)^4$ is (-2) multiplied by itself 4 times.
$(-2)^4 = (-2) \times (-2) \times (-2) \times (-2)$
-2^4 is the product of -1 and 2 multiplied by
itself 4 times.
$-2^4 = -(2 \times 2 \times 2 \times 2)$
$(-2)^4$ is positive while -2^4 is negative.

80a. b must be an even number.
b. b must be an odd number.
81. There will be 2560 plants in 2 years.

2.2 Laws of Exponents

1a. 3 ; 2 ; 5   2a. 3 ; 2 ; 1   3a. 3 ; 5 ; 15
b. 7 ; 7   b. 2 ; 2   b. 3 ; 3
4a. 2   5a. 7   6a. 1
b. 3   b. 6   b. 1

7a. 2 ; 5 ; 3^7 b. 8 ; 6 ; 4^2
c. 3 ; 4 ; 6^{12} d. 2 ; 5 ; 4^{10}
e. 2   f. 1   g. 5   h. $\frac{1}{2^5}$
i. 1   j. 1   k. $\frac{1}{4^3}$ l. $\frac{1}{3^4}$

8. 3^{2+4} ; 3^6 9. $= 5^{3+2}$
                              $= 5^5$
10. $= 6^{4+2}$ 11. $= 8^{4-3}$
    $= 6^6$ $= 8^1$
12. $= 10^{5-3}$ 13. $= 10^{5-1}$
    $= 10^2$ $= 10^4$
14. $= 2^{0+7}$ 15. $= 7^{9-0}$
    $= 2^7$ $= 7^9$
16. 2^6 17. 4^6 18. 8^{10} 19. 10^4
20. 3^8 21. 8^0 22. 9^{10} 23. 4^{30}
24. $(\frac{1}{2})^2$ 25. $(\frac{1}{5})^2$ 26. $(\frac{1}{10})^3$ 27. $(\frac{1}{6})^2$
28. $(\frac{1}{3})^3$ 29. 3^2 30. 5^3 31. $(\frac{3}{2})^2$
32. $= 4^{2+6+(-3)}$ 33. $= 8^{3+(-6)+2}$ 34. $= 7^{6-3-2}$
    $= 4^5$ $= 8^{-1}$ $= 7$
35. $= 8^{6-(-5)-(-2)}$ 36. $= 9^{3+2-4}$ 37. $= 5^{8-5+(-6)}$
    $= 8^{13}$ $= 9$ $= 5^{-3}$
38. $= 4^{0+6-(-1)}$ 39. $= 5^{6+1-(-3)}$ 40. $= 7^{6-(-1)-0}$
    $= 4^7$ $= 5^{10}$ $= 7^7$
41. $= 6^{4+(-2)+(-3)}$ 42. $= 4^{3-2-5}$ 43. $= 3^{5+(-2)-7}$
    $= 6^{-1}$ $= 4^{-4}$ $= 3^{-4}$
44. $= 3^2 \div 3^3 \times 4^2 \times 4^3$ 45. $= 3^3 \times 3^4 \times 5^6 \div 5^2$
    $= 3^{2-3} \times 4^{2+3}$ $= 3^{3+4} \times 5^{6-2}$
    $= 3^{-1} \times 4^5$ $= 3^7 \times 5^4$
46. $= 4^{-2} \div 4^3 \times 6^3 \times 6^2$ 47. $= 3^2 \times 3^0 \times 7^4 \times 7^{-1}$
    $= 4^{-2-3} \times 6^{3+2}$ $= 3^{2+0} \times 7^{4+(-1)}$
    $= 4^{-5} \times 6^5$ $= 3^2 \times 7^3$
48. $= 2^{-5} \div 2^{-3} \times 5^4 \times 5 \div 5^5$
    $= 2^{-5-(-3)} \times 5^{4+1-5}$
    $= 2^{-2} \times 5^0$
    $= 2^{-2}$
49. $= 8^{-4} \times 8^{-5} \times 9^{-3} \div 9^2 \times 9^0 \div 9^2$
    $= 8^{-4+(-5)} \times 9^{-3-2+0-2}$
    $= 8^{-9} \times 9^{-7}$
50. $= 2^5 \div 2^6 \times 3^{-3} \times 3 \times 7^2 \times 7^{-2}$
    $= 2^{5-6} \times 3^{-3+1} \times 7^{2+(-2)}$
    $= 2^{-1} \times 3^{-2} \times 7^0$
    $= 2^{-1} \times 3^{-2}$
51. $= 10^4 \times 10^{-2} \times 9^2 \times 9^3 \times 7^{-6} \div 7^2$
    $= 10^{4+(-2)} \times 9^{2+3} \times 7^{-6-2}$
    $= 10^2 \times 9^5 \times 7^{-8}$
    $= 7^{-8} \times 9^5 \times 10^2$
52a. 2^3 b. 4   c. 9^5 d. 3^{10}
e. 1   f. 8^3 g. $(-5)^5$ h. $(-2)^{-9}$
i. $(-6)^2$ j. $(-7)^{-4}$

Answers

53a. 3^{-8} b. 5^{-1} c. 4^{11} d. 1
e. $(-6)^{-5}$ f. $(-3)^{-9}$ g. 2^{-9} h. 4^2
54a. 3^8 b. 2^6 c. 2^8 d. 1
e. 3^2 f. 5   g. 2^{-3} h. 3^{-1}
i. 1   j. 7^{-3} k. 2^9 l. $\frac{2}{3}$

55. 256 coins can be stacked.

56. First, apply the negative exponent rule to rewrite $(-2)^{-3}$ as $(-\frac{1}{2})^3$. Then multiply $(-\frac{1}{2})$ by itself 3 times to get the answer of $-\frac{1}{8}$.

57. (Suggested possible ways)
Yes, $\frac{1}{64}$ can be expressed with negative exponents as 64^{-1}, 8^{-2}, 4^{-3}, 2^{-6}, $(-8)^{-2}$, and $(-2)^{-6}$, and with positive exponents as $(\frac{1}{64})^1$, $(\frac{1}{8})^2$, $(\frac{1}{4})^3$, $(\frac{1}{2})^6$, $(-\frac{1}{8})^2$, and $(-\frac{1}{2})^6$.

58. The next two Mersenne primes are 7 and 31.
59. The product of x and y can be any real number except for 0.
60. Yes, she is correct. Every integer can be expressed as itself to the power of 1 and its reciprocal to the power of -1.
e.g. $-3 = (-3)^1$
$-3 = (-\frac{1}{3})^{-1}$

2.3 Operations with Powers

1a. 6   b. 4   c. 5 ; 5   d. 8
e. 6   f. 5 ; 3
2a. 4   b. 6   c. 2 ; 2   d. 5
e. 2   f. 7 ; 4
3a. 5   b. 2   c. 3   d. 2
e. 1   f. -1
4a. 10   b. 7   c. 8   d. 5
e. 3   f. 4
5. 7   6. 3   7. 3   8. 3
9. 3   10. 6   11. 5   12. 2 ; 2
13. -2 ; -2   14. 4   15. 5   16. 4
17a. 7^4 b. 10^6 c. 6^6 d. 5^5
e. 6^2 f. $(-8)^4$
18a. 4^5 b. $7^2 \times 9^2$ c. $6^{-3} \times 8^{-3}$ d. 3
e. $(5 \times 4)^3$ f. $(-3 \times 2)^{-10}$
19a. 5 ; 6   b. $\frac{2^3}{7^3}$ c. $\frac{3^{-4}}{8^{-4}}$ d. 7 ; 3
e. $(\frac{8}{9})^3$ f. $(-\frac{4}{9})^{-5}$
20a. 27   b. -8   c. 81
d. 25   e. $\frac{1}{9}$ f. $\frac{1}{216}$

21a. $\frac{1}{9}$ b. $\frac{4}{9}$ c. $\frac{5}{4}$
d. $6\frac{1}{4}$ e. $\frac{8}{27}$ f. $\frac{9}{16}$
22a. 0.01   b. 0.25   c. 125
d. -0.008   e. -0.027   f. 0.16
23a. 2 ; 4   b. $= (2^4)^2$ c. $= (2^3)^3$
            $= 2^8$ $= 2^9$
24a. $= (3^2)^3$ b. $= (3^3)^2$ c. $= ((3^2)^2)^3$
$= 3^6$ $= 3^6$ $= 3^{12}$
25a. $= (5^2)^3$ b. $= ((5^3)^2)^2$
$= 5^6$ $= 5^{12}$
26a. $= ((-4)^2)^2$ b. $= ((-4)^3)^3$
$= (-4)^4$ $= (-4)^9$
27. $= \frac{3^4}{3^3}$ 28. $= \frac{4^5}{4^6}$ 29. $= \frac{5}{5^2}$
$= 3$ $= \frac{1}{4}$ $= \frac{1}{5}$
30. $= \frac{6^3}{6^2}$ 31. $= \frac{3^{-1}}{3^1}$ 32. $= \frac{2^9}{2^6}$
$= 6$ $= 3^{-2}$ $= 2^3$
            $= \frac{1}{9}$ $= 8$
33. $= \frac{4^4}{4^5}$ 34. $= \frac{(-2)^8}{(-2)^4}$ 35. $= (\frac{5^6}{5^4})^2$
$= \frac{1}{4}$ $= (-2)^4$ $= (5^2)^2$
            $= 16$ $= 625$
36. $= (\frac{6^4}{6^3})^3$ 37. $= (\frac{9}{9^2})^{-1}$ 38. $= \frac{7^{-8}}{7^{-7}}$
$= (6)^3$ $= (9^{-1})^{-1}$ $= 7^{-1}$
$= 216$ $= 9$ $= \frac{1}{7}$
39. $= \frac{(2^2)^2}{2^6} = \frac{2^4}{2^6} = 2^{-2} = \frac{1}{4}$
40. $= \frac{(3^2)^2(3^2)}{3^4} = \frac{3^6}{3^4} = 3^2 = 9$
41. $= \frac{((5^2)^2)^3}{5^8} = \frac{5^{12}}{5^8} = 5^4 = 625$
42. $= \frac{(2)(3^4)}{3} = 2 \times 3^3$
43. $= \frac{(3^{-2})(4^2)}{(3^5)(4^5)} = 3^{-7} \times 4^{-3}$
44. $= \frac{2^3 \times 3^3}{2^{-6} \times 3^{-2}} = 2^9 \times 3^5$
45. $= (3^2)^2 \times (2^5)^2 \times (3^3)^3 \times (2^4)^3$
$= 2^{10} \times 2^{12} \times 3^4 \times 3^9$
$= 2^{22} \times 3^{13}$
46. $= (4^2)^{-2} \times (5^3)^{-2} \times (4^3)^2 \times (5^2)^2$
$= 4^{-4} \times 4^6 \times 5^{-6} \times 5^4$
$= 4^2 \times 5^{-2}$
47. $= \frac{((-4)^2)^2 \times 5^2}{(-4)^{-4} \times 5^{-4}}$ 48. $= \frac{(7^2)^3(3^2)^3}{(3^{-2})(7^{-10})}$
$= \frac{(-4)^4 \times 5^2}{(-4)^{-4} \times 5^{-4}}$ $= \frac{(3^6)(7^6)}{(3^{-2})(7^{-10})}$
$= (-4)^8 \times 5^6$ $= 3^8 \times 7^{16}$

49. $= \dfrac{(2^5)^3(9^3)^3}{(2^5)^4(9^2)^4}$

$= \dfrac{(2^{15})(9^9)}{(2^{20})(9^8)}$

$= 2^{-5} \times 9$

50. $= \dfrac{((-3)^3)^3(5^2)^3}{((-3)^{-3})^{-2}(5^{-4})^{-2}}$

$= \dfrac{(-3)^9(5^6)}{(-3)^6(5^8)}$

$= (-3)^3 \times 5^{-2}$

51. 4 ; 2 ; 0 ; 6
52. $0 \times 2^2 + 1 \times 2^1 + 0 \times 2^0$; 8 ; 0 ; 2 ; 0 ; 10
53. $1 \times 2^3 + 0 \times 2^2 + 0 \times 2^1 + 1 \times 2^0$; 8 + 0 + 0 + 1 ; 9
54. $1 \times 2^4 + 1 \times 2^3 + 0 \times 2^2 + 1 \times 2^1 + 0 \times 2^0$

$= 16 + 8 + 0 + 2 + 0$

$= 26$

55. $1 \times 2^4 + 0 \times 2^3 + 1 \times 2^2 + 1 \times 2^1 + 1 \times 2^0$

$= 16 + 0 + 4 + 2 + 1$

$= 23$

56. $1 \times 2^4 + 0 \times 2^3 + 0 \times 2^2 + 0 \times 2^1 + 1 \times 2^0$

$= 16 + 0 + 0 + 0 + 1$

$= 17$

57. $1 \times 2^5 + 1 \times 2^4 + 0 \times 2^3 + 1 \times 2^2 + 1 \times 2^1 + 0 \times 2^0$

$= 32 + 16 + 0 + 4 + 2 + 0$

$= 54$

58. T   59. T   60. F
61. A base of 4 is equal to 2^2. The exponent in 2^8 is divisible by 2 but the exponent in 2^7 is not. Therefore, 2^8 can be expressed as a power with a base of 4, but 2^7 cannot.
62. First, rewrite the base of the power as another power. Then use the exponent rule to simplify.

e.g. $81^3 = (3^4)^3 = 3^{12}$

63a. 2, 4, 8, 64, and their reciprocals

b. 10, 100, and their reciprocals

c. 3, 9, 27, 729, and their reciprocals

64a. 18   b. 6   c. 12
65. The negative exponent rule states that a negative exponent can be expressed as a fraction with the base as the denominator. However, if the base is 0, then the denominator will be 0, which cannot be defined.
66. It is incorrect. There is a mistake in the third step.

$= \dfrac{4.5^3}{1.5^2}$

$= \dfrac{(4.5)^2(4.5)}{(1.5)^2}$

$= (\dfrac{4.5}{1.5})^2 \times 4.5$

$= 3^2 \times 4.5$

$= 40.5$

67. The cube has a side length of 2^5 cm and a surface area of $(2^{10} \times 6)$ cm^2.

68. The highest decimal number it can count to is 63.
69a. 2^6 b. 1000000

2.4 Squares and Square Roots

1a. 4   b. 10
2a. 16   b. 20
3a. 16   b. 2
4a. 4   b. 16
5a. 5   b. 4.5   c. $\dfrac{3}{4}$
6. 5   7. 8   8. 10   9. 7
10. 12   11. 3.5   12. 4   13. 8
14. 3   15. 2   16. 4   17. 3
18. 4 ; 4 ; 2
19. $= \sqrt{4 \times 5}$

$= \sqrt{4} \times \sqrt{5}$

$= 2\sqrt{5}$

20. $= \sqrt{9 \times 3}$

$= \sqrt{9} \times \sqrt{3}$

$= 3\sqrt{3}$

21. $= \sqrt{25 \times 2}$

$= \sqrt{25} \times \sqrt{2}$

$= 5\sqrt{2}$

22. $= \sqrt{16 \times 2}$

$= \sqrt{16} \times \sqrt{2}$

$= 4\sqrt{2}$

23. $= \sqrt{9 \times 6}$

$= \sqrt{9} \times \sqrt{6}$

$= 3\sqrt{6}$

24. $= \sqrt{16 \times 3}$

$= \sqrt{16} \times \sqrt{3}$

$= 4\sqrt{3}$

25. $\sqrt{36 \times 2} = \sqrt{36} \times \sqrt{2} = 6\sqrt{2}$
26. $\sqrt{4 \times 30} = \sqrt{4} \times \sqrt{30} = 2\sqrt{30}$
27. $\sqrt{25 \times 6} = \sqrt{25} \times \sqrt{6} = 5\sqrt{6}$
28. $\sqrt{100 \times 2} = \sqrt{100} \times \sqrt{2} = 10\sqrt{2}$
29. $\sqrt{81 \times 3} = \sqrt{81} \times \sqrt{3} = 9\sqrt{3}$
30. $\sqrt{121 \times 3} = \sqrt{121} \times \sqrt{3} = 11\sqrt{3}$
31. $= 2\sqrt{3} \times 2\sqrt{2} = 4\sqrt{6}$
32. $= 4\sqrt{2} \times 3\sqrt{2} = 12 \times 2 = 24$
33. $= 2\sqrt{5} \times \sqrt{2} \times \sqrt{5} = 10\sqrt{2}$
34. $= 3\sqrt{6} \times 2 \times \sqrt{6} \times \sqrt{4} = 3 \times 6 \times 2 \times 2 = 72$
35. $= \sqrt{8} \times \sqrt{10} \div \sqrt{10} = \sqrt{4 \times 2} = 2\sqrt{2}$
36. $= 3\sqrt{6} \div \sqrt{6} \div \sqrt{3} = \dfrac{3}{\sqrt{3}}$
37. $= \sqrt{\dfrac{3}{4} \times \dfrac{2}{9}} = \dfrac{1}{\sqrt{6}}$
38. $= \sqrt{\dfrac{4}{5} \times 20} = \sqrt{16} = 4$
39. $= \sqrt{150} \div \sqrt{9 \times 5} = \sqrt{\dfrac{150}{45}} = \sqrt{\dfrac{10}{3}}$
40. $= \sqrt{25 \times 2} \div \sqrt{4 \times 5} = \sqrt{\dfrac{50}{20}} = \sqrt{\dfrac{5}{2}}$
41. $= 2 \times 3 \times \sqrt{8} \times \sqrt{2} \div 2 = 3 \times \sqrt{16} = 3 \times 4 = 12$
42. $= \dfrac{\sqrt{125}}{\sqrt{125 \times 2}} = \dfrac{1}{\sqrt{2}}$
43. $= \dfrac{2\sqrt{2} \times 4\sqrt{3}}{8\sqrt{15}} = \sqrt{\dfrac{6}{15}} = \sqrt{\dfrac{2}{5}}$
44a. $7\sqrt{6}$ b. -12   c. -12

d. 1   e. 5   f. $6\sqrt{2}$

Answers

45. No, he is incorrect. While the square of $\sqrt{-2}$ equals -2, numbers that have square roots must be positive or 0. -2 is a negative number, so it does not have a square root.

46. $\sqrt{a^2}$
$= \sqrt{a \times a}$
$= \sqrt{a} \times \sqrt{a}$
$= a$

47. (Suggested answers)
a. $a = 4, b = 9$
$\sqrt{4 + 9} = \sqrt{13}$
$\sqrt{4} + \sqrt{9} = 2 + 3 = 5$
So, $\sqrt{a + b} \neq \sqrt{a} + \sqrt{b}$.
b. $a = 9, b = 4$
$\sqrt{9 - 4} = \sqrt{5}$
$\sqrt{9} - \sqrt{4} = 3 - 2 = 1$
So, $\sqrt{a - b} \neq \sqrt{a} - \sqrt{b}$.
c. $a = 2, b = 3$
$\sqrt{2^2 + 3^2} = \sqrt{13}$
$2 + 3 = 5$
So, $\sqrt{a^2 + b^2} \neq a + b$.

48. The square root of a negative number cannot be evaluated because no integer multiplied by itself can result in a negative number.
e.g. $\sqrt{-4} = ?$
$2 \times 2 = 4$
$(-2) \times (-2) = 4$
So, it cannot be evaluated.

49a. The side length of the garden is $5\sqrt{2}$ m.
b. The perimeter of the garden is $20\sqrt{2}$ m.

50a. The surface area is $(20\sqrt{2} + 12\sqrt{5} + 12\sqrt{10})$ m^2.
b. The volume is 60 m^3.

51a. The length of the hypotenuse is $5\sqrt{6}$ m.
b. The perimeter is $(10\sqrt{3} + 5\sqrt{6})$ m.

2.5 Scientific Notation

1a. 3
b. 4.32
$4\,3\,2\,0\,0.$
4 3 2 1
c. 4
$9\,0\,2\,7\,1.$
4 3 2 1

d. 3.60028
$3\,6\,0\,0\,2\,8.$
5 4 3 2 1
e. 5
$5\,2\,0\,1\,0\,0.$
5 4 3 2 1
f. 1.02047
$1\,0\,2\,0\,4\,7.$
5 4 3 2 1

2a. -1
b. 7.23
$0.7\,2\,3$
1
c. -2
$0.0\,8\,4$
1 2

d. 4.9
$0.0\,0\,4\,9$
1 2 3
e. -4
$0.0\,0\,0\,9\,2\,4$
1 2 3 4
f. 5.1
$0.0\,0\,0\,0\,5\,1$
1 2 3 4 5

3. 5×10^3
4. 4×10^{-2}
5. 5.2×10^{-2}
6. 2.408×10^4
7. 3.007×10^5
8. -4.09×10^{-2}
9. 8×10^{-3}
10. 1.085×10^6

11. -2.45×10^{-4}
12. 7.9031×10^6
13a. 300
b. 2200
c. 40 500
d. -512 000
14a. 0.06
b. 0.0091
c. 0.0001743
d. -0.00008
15. 2.5×10^{-1}
16. 8×10^{-4}
17. ✔
18. 1×10^3
19. 6.6×10^3
20. 5.9×10^0
21. ✔
22. -1.1×10^4
23. 1×10^2
24. 9×10^{-1}
25. <
26. >
27. <
28. >
29. <
30. =
31. <
32. <
33. >
34. =
35. 5×3 ; 1.5
36. $= 4 \div 5 \times 10^2$
$= 8 \times 10^1$
37. $= 7 \times 2 \times 10^{-2}$
$= 1.4 \times 10^{-1}$
38. $= 8 \div 20 \times 10^{-1}$
$= 4 \times 10^{-2}$
39. $= 1.2 \times 3 \times 10^3 \times 10^2$
$= 3.6 \times 10^5$
40. $= -2.5 \div 5 \times 10^2 \div 10^1 = -5 \times 10^0$
41. $= 3.6 \times 4 \times 10^{-3} \times 10^2 = 1.44 \times 10^0$
42. $= 4.2 \div 7 \times 10^3 \div 10^{-1} = 6 \times 10^3$
43. $= -8.6 \div 4 \times 10^{-4} \div 10^2 = -2.15 \times 10^{-6}$
44. $= 1.25 \div 5 \times 10^5 \div 10^{-2} = 2.5 \times 10^6$
45. $= 4.5 \times (-2.5) \times 10^{-2} \times 10^6 = -1.125 \times 10^5$
46. $= 8.1 \div 9 \times 10^5 \div 10^{-3} = 9 \times 10^7$
47a. 3×10^{-1}
b. 2.5×10^{-1}
c. 1×10^2
d. 2.43×10^2
e. 6.25×10^2
f. 1.25×10^{-1}
48. $-1.2 \times 10^4 < -3.4 \times 10^{-1} < 5.07 \times 10^{-3} < 8.9 \times 10^2$
49a. False. A number with a greater value of a but a smaller value of n can be smaller.
e.g. $1.5 \times 10^2 > 2 \times 10^1$
b. False. The sign (positive or negative) of a can determine which is greater.
e.g. $9.9 \times 10^2 > -1 \times 10^3$
50. Writing numbers with powers of 10 allows for easier conversion between decimal numbers because digits in decimal numbers are 10 times the value of the digit on the right.
e.g. 150 in powers of 10:
Move the decimal two places to the left. The exponent of the power is 2.
$150 = 1.5 \times 10^2$
150 in powers of 2:
Divide 150 by 2 until a number between 1 and 10 remains.
$150 \div 2 = 75$
$75 \div 2 = 37.5$
$37.5 \div 2 = 18.75$
$18.75 \div 2 = 9.375$
Divided 150 by 2 four times, so the exponent of the power is 4.
$150 = 9.375 \times 2^4$

51. The volume of Earth is about 50 times that of the moon.

52. A virus particle is about 300 times as large as an oxygen molecule.

53. The population of Canada was approximately 3.7×10^7.

54a. The speed of light is approximately 3×10^8 m/s.

b. It takes about 495 seconds or 8 minutes and 15 seconds for light to travel to Earth from the sun.

55. The average change was $\$3.5225 \times 10^5$ per quarter.

Quiz 2

1. B 2. D 3. B 4. B
5. B 6. D 7. C
8. T 9. F 10. F 11. T
12a. F b. F c. T

13. $2^3 \times 3^2$

14. $3^2 \times 5^2$

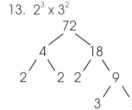

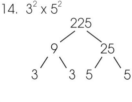

15. $2^2 \times 7^2$

16. $3^3 \times 5^2$

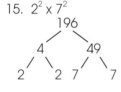

17. 2^8 18. $(-3)^2$ 19. 5^1 20. $(-2)^3$
21. 8^{-1} 22. $(-7)^3$ 23. 3^8 24. 10^{-4}
25. 2^2 26. 3^{-1} 27. 5^{12} 28. 6^0 or 1

29-40. (Suggested answers)

29. 2^4 30. 10^3 31. $(-3)^3$ 32. 3^8
33. $(\frac{1}{5})^9$ 34. $(\frac{1}{6})^{10}$ 35. $(\frac{5}{3})^2$ 36. $(\frac{1}{11})^3$
37. $(\frac{6}{7})^3$ 38. 2^2 39. 7^3 40. $(\frac{1}{2})^3$

41. $= 3^{5 + 2 - 3}$
$= 3^4$

42. $= 4^{3 - (-1) + 6}$
$= 4^{10}$

43. $= 2^{-6} \div 2^{-2} \times 2^3$
$= 2^{-6 - (-2) + 3}$
$= 2^{-1}$

44. $= 6^2 \times 6^6$
$= 6^{2 + 6}$
$= 6^8$

45. $= 3^3 \times 3^{-2} \div 3^4$
$= 3^{3 + (-2) - 4}$
$= 3^{-3}$

46. $= 5^3 \div 5^2 \times 5^{-2}$
$= 5^{3 - 2 + (-2)}$
$= 5^{-1}$

47. $= (\frac{1.2}{3})^2$
$= (0.4)^2$
$= 0.16$

48. $= \sqrt{4} \times \sqrt{6} \times \sqrt{6}$
$= 2 \times 6$
$= 12$

49. $= \sqrt{20} \times \sqrt{10} \div \sqrt{10} = \sqrt{4} \times \sqrt{5} = 2\sqrt{5}$

50. $= 4\sqrt{2} \div 2\sqrt{2} = 2$ 51. $= \frac{2 \times 4 \times 3 \times \sqrt{2}}{4 \times \sqrt{2}} = 6$

52. $= \frac{2 \times \sqrt{3} \times \sqrt{5} \times \sqrt{2} \times \sqrt{5}}{\sqrt{2} \times 3 \times \sqrt{3} \times \sqrt{9}} = \frac{2 \times 5}{3 \times 3} = 1\frac{1}{9}$

53. $2^6 \div 4 \div 2^{-4} = 2^6 \div 2^2 \div 2^{-4} = 2^{6 - 2 - (-4)} = 2^8$
One section can store 2^8 files.

54. $30 \div 3\sqrt{2}$
$= 10 \div \sqrt{2}$
$= \sqrt{100} \div \sqrt{2}$
$= \sqrt{50}$
$= 5\sqrt{2}$
The length of the rug is $5\sqrt{2}$ m.

55. $(9.2 \times 10^8) \div (5.75 \times 10^6)$
$= 9.2 \div 5.75 \times 10^8 \div 10^6$
$= 1.6 \times 10^2$
$= 160$
The movie was at the box office for 160 days.

56a. $(1.07496 \times 10^{23}) \div (5.972 \times 10^{24})$
$= 1.07496 \div 5.972 \times 10^{23} \div 10^{24}$
$= 0.18 \times 10^{-1}$
$= 0.018$
$= 1.8\%$
1.8% of Earth's mass comes from nickel.

b. $5.972 \times 10^{24} \times 30\%$
$= 5.972 \times 10^{24} \times 0.3$
$= 1.7916 \times 10^{24}$
The oxygen on Earth weighs 1.7916×10^{24} kg.

57. $\sqrt{(\sqrt{5})^2 - (\frac{3}{\sqrt{2}})^2} = \sqrt{5 - \frac{9}{2}} = \sqrt{\frac{1}{2}} = \frac{1}{\sqrt{2}}$
The length of the third side is $\frac{1}{\sqrt{2}}$ m.

58. $(2^4)^2 \div 2^6 = 2^{8-6} = 2^2 = 4$
The area is 4 cm².

59. First, identify the decimal point and move it to the left or right until the magnitude of the decimal is between 1 and 10 (excluding 10). Then determine a power of 10 with an exponent that is equal to the number of places the decimal point moved. If it was moved to the left, the exponent is positive, and if it was moved to the right, the exponent is negative.

60. Consider b as an integer.
$a^b \times a^{-b} = a^b \times \frac{1}{a^b}$
$a^{b + (-b)} = \frac{a^b}{a^b}$
$a^0 = 1$

61. Consider b as an integer.
$a^{b + 1} \div a^b = \frac{a^{b+1}}{a^b}$
$a^{b + 1 - b} = \frac{a^b \times a}{a^b}$
$a^1 = a$

Answers

62. The product of any number multiplied by itself is always positive, despite whether the number is positive or negative. Since no number multiplied by itself can result in a negative number, a negative number cannot be a squared number.

63a. $= \sqrt{16}$
  $= 4$

b. $= \sqrt{(2^2)^3}$
  $= \sqrt{(2^3)^2}$
  $= 2^3$
  $= 8$

c. $= (\sqrt{400} \times \sqrt{2} \div 5)^{-2}$
  $= (20\sqrt{2} \div 5)^{-2}$
  $= (4\sqrt{2})^{-2}$
  $= (\frac{1}{4\sqrt{2}})^2$
  $= \frac{1}{16 \times 2}$
  $= \frac{1}{32}$

64. $(a^6)^2 \times (a^3)^{-5}$ simplifies to a^{-3}. Since the power has a negative exponent and a base greater than 1, its answer must take the form of a fraction with a numerator of 1 and a denominator greater than 1. Therefore, the value of the expression must be less than 1.

Chapter 3: Algebra

3.1 Algebraic Expressions

1a. 10   b. 16   c. 1   d. 9
  e. -5   f. -2   g. 4 ; 4   h. -3 ; 3
2a. 5   b. 6   c. 16   d. 5
  e. 3   f. 3   g. 1   h. 7
3a. 5   b. 6   c. 7   d. 2
  e. 4   f. 2   g. 7   h. 2
4. $12x$ 5. $-16x$ 6. x^6 7. $5x$
8. $6x^3$ 9. $7x^4$ 10. $-2x^2$ 11. x
12. $x + 6$ 13. $3x^2$ 14. $6x$ 15. $-x^2 + 15$
16. $4x$ 17. x 18. $x^3 - 2$
19. $= 3(3x)$ 20. $= x(2x)$ 21. $= x^3$
  $= 9x$ $= 2x^2$
22. $= 5x^4$ 23. $= -6(4x)$ 24. $= 2x^2(3x^2)$
         $= -24x$ $= 6x^4$
25. $= 2x(x)$ 26. $= \sqrt{x^2}(x)$ 27. $= (x^{-2})(x^2)$
  $= 2x^2$ $= x(x)$ $= x^0$
           $= x^2$ $= 1$
28. $= x^4(4x^2)$ 29. $= 3x(9x^2)$ 30. $= x^6(3x)$
  $= 4x^6$ $= 27x^3$ $= 3x^7$
31a. $4(2)$ b. $-8 \div (2)$ c. $(2)^2$
  $= 8$ $= -4$ $= 4$
  d. $(2)^3 - 1$
   $= 8 - 1$
   $= 7$

32a. $7(-1)$ b. $(-1)^3 + 1$ c. $-((-1)^2) - 6$
  $= -7$ $= -1 + 1$ $= -1 - 6$
        $= 0$ $= -7$
33a. $2(-2)^2$ b. $(\sqrt{-2 \times (-2)})^2$ c. $(-2)^2(-2 + 3)$
  $= 2(4)$ $= (\sqrt{4})^2$ $= 4(1)$
  $= 8$ $= 4$ $= 4$
34a. $4(1)^2$ b. $4(3)^2$
  $= 4$ $= 4(9)$
        $= 36$
35a. $3(2^2)^3$ b. $3((-1)^2)^3$ c. $3((-2)^2)^3$
  $= 3(2^6)$ $= 3(1^3)$ $= 3(-2)^6$
  $= 3(64)$ $= 3$ $= 3(64)$
  $= 192$ $= 192$
36a. $2(3) + 3(-1)$ b. $-4(3^2 + (-1))$
  $= 6 + (-3)$ $= -4(9 - 1)$
  $= 3$ $= -4(8)$
          $= -32$
37a. $10 - (-2)^2$ b. $((10)^2(-2))^3$
  $= 10 - 4$ $= (-200)^3$
  $= 6$ $= -8\,000\,000$
38a. $4(-3) + 4$ b. $6((-3)^2 - \sqrt{4})$
  $= -12 + 4$ $= 6(9 - 2)$
  $= -8$ $= 6(7)$
          $= 42$
39. $= 2(3x)$ 40. $= x(5x)$
  $= 6x$ $= 5x^2$
  $6(3) = 18$ $5(-3)^2 = 5(9) = 45$
41. $= 2x^5$
  $2(-2)^5 = 2(-32) = -64$
42. $= (2x)(x)$ 43. $= (x)^2(3x^2)$
  $= 2x^2$ $= 3x^4$
  $2(5)^2 = 2(25) = 50$ $3(2^4) = 3(16) = 48$
44a. $2x + 3$
  $x + 2x + 3 = 3x + 3$
  b. for $x = 1$, $3(1) + 3 = 6$; 6 hours
   for $x = 3$, $3(3) + 3 = 12$; 12 hours
45a. $x^2 + (3x)^2$
  $= x^2 + 9x^2$
  $= 10x^2$
  b. for $x = 2$, $10(2^2) = 10(4) = 40$; 40 cm^2
   for $x = 5$, $10(5^2) = 10(25) = 250$; 250 cm^2
46. The values of x cannot be less than 0 because both hours worked and the side length of a square must be a positive number.
47. F   48. F   49. F   50. T   51. F
52a. a^4 b. $3x^8$ c. $9y^2$ d. $16n^4$
  e. $6i$ f. $-6a^4$ g. $-5s^2$ h. $2m^4$
53a. 1   b. -1   c. -10   d. 15
  e. $-\frac{1}{9}$ f. 0.01   g. 0   h. $2\frac{26}{27}$

54a. x^2 ; 16   b. b^4 ; 81   c. $-3m^3$; -24

   d. $\dfrac{1}{a^9}$; $-\dfrac{1}{512}$

55. Eva's solution is correct and Howard's is incorrect. When substituting -2 for x, the negative sign must also be included to be squared.

56. When $a = 5$ and $b = 2.5$, the denominator $a - 2b$ is equal to 0 and fractions with a denominator of 0 are undefined.

57a. The surface area is 600 cm^2.
   b. The surface area is 12 150 cm^2.
   c. The surface area is 34.56 cm^2.

58. The area of the circle is 120.7016 cm^2.

59a. $\dfrac{3}{4}x^2$ b. The volume is 27 cubic units.

3.2 Algebraic Equations

1. 10 ; 5
2. 4 ; 36
3. 1 ; 12 ; 12 ; 2 ; 6
4. 2 ; 3 ; 3 ; 18
5. 2 ; 6 ; 6 ; 3 ; 2
6. 2 ; 3 ; 3 ; 1 ; 4

7. $4x - 2 + 2 = 10 + 2$
   $4x = 12$
   $4x \div 4 = 12 \div 4$
   $x = 3$

8. $9 + 2x - 9 = 15 - 9$
   $2x = 6$
   $2x \div 2 = 6 \div 2$
   $x = 3$

9. $3(x - 2) \div 3 = 9 \div 3$
   $x - 2 = 3$
   $x - 2 + 2 = 3 + 2$
   $x = 5$

10. $\dfrac{2x}{3} \times 3 = 8 \times 3$
   $2x = 24$
   $2x \div 2 = 24 \div 2$
   $x = 12$

11. $\dfrac{x + 1}{4} \times 4 = 6 \times 4$
   $x + 1 = 24$
   $x + 1 - 1 = 24 - 1$
   $x = 23$

12. $5x - 3 + 3 = -8 + 3$
   $5x = -5$
   $5x \div 5 = -5 \div 5$
   $x = -1$

13. $-2(x + 3) \div -2 = -10 \div -2$
   $x + 3 = 5$
   $x + 3 - 3 = 5 - 3$
   $x = 2$

14. $\dfrac{4}{5}x + 6 - 6 = -2 - 6$
   $\dfrac{4}{5}x = -8$
   $\dfrac{4}{5}x \div \dfrac{4}{5} = -8 \div \dfrac{4}{5}$
   $x = -8 \times \dfrac{5}{4}$
   $x = -10$

15. $-\dfrac{x + 1}{3} \times -3 = 1 \times -3$
   $x + 1 = -3$
   $x + 1 - 1 = -3 - 1$
   $x = -4$

16. $10 - 3x - 10 = 4 - 10$
   $-3x = -6$
   $-3x \div -3 = -6 \div -3$
   $x = 2$

17. $\sqrt{x} + 1 = 3$
   $\sqrt{x} + 1 - 1 = 3 - 1$
   $\sqrt{x} = 2$
   $(\sqrt{x})^2 = 2^2$
   $x = 4$

18. $2\sqrt{x} \div 2 = 6 \div 2$
   $\sqrt{x} = 3$
   $(\sqrt{x})^2 = 3^2$
   $x = 9$

19. $\dfrac{\sqrt{x} - 1}{5} \times 5 = 1 \times 5$
   $\sqrt{x} - 1 = 5$
   $\sqrt{x} - 1 + 1 = 5 + 1$
   $\sqrt{x} = 6$
   $(\sqrt{x})^2 = 6^2$
   $x = 36$

20. $3\sqrt{x} - 2 + 2 = 10 + 2$
   $3\sqrt{x} = 12$
   $3\sqrt{x} \div 3 = 12 \div 3$
   $\sqrt{x} = 4$
   $(\sqrt{x})^2 = 4^2$
   $x = 16$

21. $2x - 5 = 3$
   $2x = 8$
   $x = 4$

22. $3(x + 1) = 9$
   $x + 1 = 3$
   $x = 2$

23. $4 + \dfrac{2}{3}x = 8$
   $\dfrac{2}{3}x = 4$
   $x = 6$

24. $\dfrac{1}{4}(6 + x) = 2$
   $6 + x = 8$
   $x = 2$

25. $7 - 3x = -2$
   $-3x = -9$
   $x = 3$

26. $-2(x - 1) = -6$
   $x - 1 = 3$
   $x = 4$

27. $10 + \sqrt{x} = 13$
   $\sqrt{x} = 3$
   $(\sqrt{x})^2 = 3^2$
   $x = 9$

28. $\sqrt{x} + 9 = 13$
   $\sqrt{x} = 4$
   $(\sqrt{x})^2 = 4^2$
   $x = 16$

29. $\dfrac{1}{5}\sqrt{x} = 1$
   $\sqrt{x} = 5$
   $(\sqrt{x})^2 = 5^2$
   $x = 25$

30. $\sqrt{2x} = 4$
   $(\sqrt{2x})^2 = 4^2$
   $2x = 16$
   $x = 8$

31a. 4   b. 4   c. 8   d. -1
   e. -2   f. -10

32a. 4   b. 9   c. 4   d. 100
   e. 25   f. 4

33a. 2   b. -2   c. 5   d. $\dfrac{1}{3}$
   e. 3   f. $\dfrac{1}{5}$

34a. 1   b. 10.5   c. 10   d. 2.5
   e. 27   f. 7   g. 6.8   h. -22.5

35. Both their solutions are incorrect. Dave cannot divide 4 from the left side within the square root (see the third step). Tom did not resolve the square root correctly (see the second step).
   Correct solution:
   $\sqrt{4x} + 1 = 5$
   $\sqrt{4x} = 4$
   $(\sqrt{4x})^2 = 4^2$
   $4x = 16$
   $x = 4$

Answers

36. Yes, she is correct. There is only one solution, which is -3. There is no other number that can satisfy this equation.
37. No, he is incorrect. Since x is squared, there can be two solutions. x is either 3 or -3.
38. Since each variable can take on multiple values, the solutions can vary.
    e.g. $x + y = 10$
    If $x = 1$, then $y = 9$.
    If $x = 2$, then $y = 8$.

3.3 Problem Solving Using Algebra (1)

1a. 5   b. 14   c. 8
    $h = 35 \div 5$ $b = 14 \div 3.5$ $A = 20$
    $h = 7$ $b = 4$

2a. 6   b. 21   c. 0.25
    $15 = l + 6$ $10.5 = 7 + w$ $P = 20.5$
    $l = 15 - 6$ $w = 10.5 - 7$
    $l = 9$ $w = 3.5$

3. $A = bh \div 2$
   a. $20 = 4h \div 2$ b. $16 = 8b \div 2$
      $2h = 20$ $4b = 16$
      $h = 10$ $b = 4$

4. $A = (a + b)h \div 2$
   a. $9 = (a + 4)3 \div 2$
       $18 = (a + 4)3$
       $a + 4 = 6$
       $a = 2$
   b. $15 = (2.5 + 5)h \div 2$
      $30 = 7.5h$
      $h = 30 \div 7.5$
      $h = 4$

5. $C = 2\pi r$
   a. $18.84 = 2 \times 3.14 \times r$
          $r = 18.84 \div 2 \div 3.14$
          $r = 3$
   b. $C = 2 \times 3.14 \times 2.5$
      $C = 15.7$

6. $V = lwh$
   a. $112 = l \times 4 \times 7$ b. $48 = 5 \times 1.2 \times h$
      $l = 112 \div 4 \div 7$ $h = 48 \div 5 \div 1.2$
      $l = 4$ $h = 8$

7. $2m + 5 = 17$ 8. $4(p - 1) = 26$
   $2m = 12$ $p - 1 = 6.5$
   $m = 6$ $p = 7.5$
   m is 6. p is 7.5.

9. $2t + 1 = -10$ 10. $\dfrac{(d + 2)}{3} = 4$
   $2t = -11$ $d + 2 = 12$
   $t = -5.5$ $d = 10$
   t is -5.5. d is 10.

11. $\dfrac{c}{2} + 6 = 21$
    $\dfrac{c}{2} = 15$
    $c = 30$
    c is 30.

12. $\dfrac{6}{5} = \dfrac{2 + e}{10}$
    $5(2 + e) = 6 \times 10$
    $2 + e = 12$
    $e = 10$
    10 more eggs are needed.

13. $4\sqrt{a} = 36$
    $\sqrt{a} = 9$
    $(\sqrt{a})^2 = 9^2$
    $a = 81$
    a is 81.

14. $\dfrac{1}{6} = \dfrac{8}{12d}$
    $12d = 6 \times 8$
    $d = 4$
    d is 4.

15a. 100°C   b. 0°C   c. -25°C   d. 95°F
  e. 158°F   f. 23°F

16a. $l = \dfrac{A}{w}$ b. $l = 25$
    $w = \dfrac{P}{2} - l$ $w = 7\dfrac{5}{8}$
    $b = \dfrac{2A}{h}$ $b = \dfrac{2\sqrt{5}}{\sqrt{2}}$
    $r = \dfrac{C}{2\pi}$ $r = 0.01$
    $h = \dfrac{V}{\pi r^2}$ $h = 0.5$

17. Allen's equation is incorrect. He should have put a square root over a instead of squaring it. Michael's equation is correct but he made a mistake in solving it.
    Correct solution:
    $4\sqrt{a} + 10 = 34$
        $4\sqrt{a} = 24$
         $\sqrt{a} = 6$
       $(\sqrt{a})^2 = 6^2$
              $a = 36$
    a is 36.

3.4 Problem Solving Using Algebra (2)

1. 3.5   2. 12 ; 50
   $x = 10.5 \div 3.5$ $12x = 36.6$
   $x = 3$ $x = 3.05$
   3   3.05

3. the number of minutes it takes
   $8x = 400$
    $x = 50$
   It will take 50 minutes.

4. Let x be the car's price.
   $0.13x = 1560$
       $x = 12\,000$
   The car's price was $12 000.

5. Let x be the original bill.
   $0.2x = 3$
      $x = 15$
   The original bill was $15.

6. Let x be the number of batteries in each pack.
$$3x - 9 = 15$$
$$3x = 24$$
$$x = 8$$
There were 8 batteries in each pack.

7. Let x be the number of cups of milk needed.
$$\frac{x}{5} = \frac{\frac{3}{4}}{3}$$
$$3x = 5 \times \frac{3}{4}$$
$$x = 1\frac{1}{4}$$
$1\frac{1}{4}$ cups of milk are needed.

8. Let x be the number of towelettes in a regular pack.
$$10(x - 20) = 100$$
$$x - 20 = 10$$
$$x = 30$$
There are 30 towelettes in a regular pack.

9. Let x be the number of trees before.
$$(x + 8) \div 2 = 25$$
$$x + 8 = 50$$
$$x = 42$$
There were 42 trees before.

10. Let x be the number of nickels.
$$0.1(50) + 0.05x = 6.25$$
$$5 + 0.05x = 6.25$$
$$0.05x = 1.25$$
$$x = 25$$
There are 25 nickels.

11. Let x be the amount he withdrew.
$$\frac{3}{4}(40 + x) = 75$$
$$40 + x = 100$$
$$x = 60$$
He withdrew $60.

12. Let x be the amount of time the return trip took.
$$1.2(60)x = 1\frac{1}{2} \times 60$$
$$72x = 90$$
$$x = 1\frac{1}{4}$$
The return trip took $1\frac{1}{4}$ h.

13. Let x be the number of bags.
$$(210 \div x) - 5 = 25$$
$$210 \div x = 30$$
$$x = 7$$
There are 7 bags.

14. Let x be the balance on the gift card.
$$\frac{3}{5}x + 25 = 55$$
$$\frac{3}{5}x = 30$$
$$x = 50$$
The balance on the gift card was $50.

15a. $x = 2y + 6$
  b. $3x = \frac{y + 5}{2}$

16. (Suggested answers)
  a. $8x + 1.8(10) = 30$
  b. $4\sqrt{a} = 56$
  c. $0.02(300)t = 36$

17a. He took 3 marbles from each bag.
  b. Its width is 8 cm.
  c. Its base is 15 cm and its height is 24 cm.
  d. He has 40 quarters and 100 dimes.

Quiz 3

1. C
2. D
3. D
4. B
5. B
6. A
7. B
8. $16x$
9. $-21e$
10. $45c^2$
11. $-4a$
12. b^6
13. $3m^{-3}$
14. $16c$
15. $4d$
16. $14x^2$
17. $\frac{7}{10}n^3$

18. $= 4(3c)$
$= 12c$
$12(1) = 12$

19. $= 2x^4$
$2(2^4) = 2^5 = 32$

20. $= -7(-3n)$
$= 21n$
$21(-2) = -42$

21. $= 9p^4$
$9(3^4) = 9(81) = 729$

22. $= -8r^{-3}$
$-8(-3)^{-3} = \frac{8}{3^3} = \frac{8}{27}$

23. $= 5y(-y)$
$= -5y^2$
$-5(10^2) = -500$

24. $= -k^2(-k^2)$
$= k^4$
$3^4 = 81$

25. $= 2m(4m^2)$
$= 8m^3$
$8(\frac{1}{2})^3 = \frac{8}{8} = 1$

26. $= s^{-6}(2s)$
$= 2s^{-5}$
$2(-1)^{-5} = -2$

27. $4a = 8$
$a = 2$

28. $\frac{2}{5}d = 4$
$d = 10$

29. $2k = 6$
$k = 3$

30. $h - 1 = -2$
$h = -1$

31. $4c = 72$
$c = 18$

32. $2x + 1 = 3$
$2x = -4$
$x = -2$

33. $4n = 108$
$n = 27$

Answers

34. $3(r + 1) = 10$
$$r + 1 = \frac{10}{3}$$
$$r = 2\frac{1}{3}$$

35. $5k - k = 13 + 11$
$$4k = 24$$
$$k = 6$$

36. $(\frac{bh}{2})t$
$$60 = (\frac{10 \times 6}{2})t$$
$$60 = 30t$$
$$t = 2$$

37. $\pi r^2 h$
$$127.17 = 3.14 \times 3^2 \times h$$
$$h = 127.17 \div 3.14 \div 9$$
$$h = 4.5$$

38a. $7d + 6$

b. $90

39a. $\frac{9 + e}{2}$

b. 7 eggs

40. Let x be her spending last month.
$$0.3x = 135$$
$$x = 135 \div 0.3$$
$$x = 450$$
Her spending last month was $450.

41. Let x be the number of orders delivered.
$$3.5x + 22.5 = 75$$
$$3.5x = 52.5$$
$$x = 15$$
He delivered 15 orders.

42. Let x be Ivy's savings.
$$\frac{4}{5}x + 8 = 68$$
$$\frac{4}{5}x = 60$$
$$x = 75$$
Ivy's savings was $75.

43. Let x be the number of quarters.
$$0.25x + 0.05(7) = 2.6$$
$$0.25x + 0.35 = 2.6$$
$$0.25x = 2.25$$
$$x = 9$$
There are 9 quarters.

44. Let x be the height.
$$(x)(2x) \div 2 = 169$$
$$2x^2 \div 2 = 169$$
$$x^2 = 169$$
$$x = \sqrt{169}$$
$$x = 13$$
The height is 13 cm.

45. Simplifying an algebraic expression reduces the number of steps needed to evaluate it. Often, some operations will cancel out. It will also be less likely to compute large numbers when an expression is simplified.

46. $(x - 4)^2$ cannot be 0, and therefore, x cannot be 4. This is important because a fraction with the denominator of 0 is undefined.

47a. $2x - 1 = 9^2$
$$2x = 82$$
$$x = 41$$

b. $\sqrt{4x} \times \sqrt{x} = 8 \times 5$
$$2x = 40$$
$$x = 20$$

c. $\frac{x^2 + x^2}{x} = 3x - 1$
$$\frac{2x^2}{x} = 3x - 1$$
$$2x = 3x - 1$$
$$3x - 2x = 1$$
$$x = 1$$

d. $x - \frac{1}{4} = 2^2 \times 5$
$$x = 20 + \frac{1}{4}$$
$$x = 20\frac{1}{4}$$

e. $3^2 x = (\frac{1}{2})^2(x + 1)$
$$9x = \frac{1}{4}x + \frac{1}{4}$$
$$9x - \frac{1}{4}x = \frac{1}{4}$$
$$8\frac{3}{4}x = \frac{1}{4}$$
$$x = \frac{1}{35}$$

f. $x(x - 2)^2 = x(x - 2)$
$$\frac{x(x - 2)^2}{x(x - 2)} = \frac{x(x - 2)}{x(x - 2)}$$
$$x - 2 = 1$$
$$x = 3$$

48a. Let x be Tony's age last year.
$$x + 18 + 1 = 4(x + 1)$$
$$x + 19 = 4x + 4$$
$$4x - x = 19 - 4$$
$$3x = 15$$
$$x = 5$$
Last year, Tony was 5 years old.

b. Let x be the width of the rectangle.
$$2x(x) = x^2 + 25$$
$$2x^2 = x^2 + 25$$
$$2x^2 - x^2 = 25$$
$$x^2 = 25$$
$$x = 5$$
The width of the rectangle is 5 cm.

Chapter 4: Polynomials

4.1 Introduction to Polynomials

1. B
2. T
3. B
4. M
5. M
6. T
7. T
8. B
9. B
10. M
11. M
12. B
13. T
14. M
15. T

16a. 2
   Degree: 2

b. 2 ; 1
   Degree: 2

c. 3 ; 1 ; 2 ; 2
   Degree: 3

d. 2 ; 4 ; 0 ; 5
   Degree: 5

e. 4 ; 6 ; 4 ; 1
   Degree: 6

f. 5 ; 7 ; 0
   Degree: 7

17a. binomial ; 1   b. binomial ; 2
c. binomial ; 3   d. trinomial ; 2
e. monomial ; 4   f. trinomial ; 4
g. trinomial ; 4   h. binomial ; 5
18. A ; D   19. A ; D   20. B ; D
21. B ; D   22. A ; D   23. B ; D
24. $x^2 + 6x$ 25. $2x^2 + x + 10$
26. $-3x^2 + x + 1$ 27. $x^3 - 2x^2 + 5$
28. $-x^2 - 5x + 12$ 29. $x^2y + 3x^2 + 7y$
30. $-xy^2 + y^2 + y$ 31. $x^2y - xy - 9x$
32. $x^2y^2 - x^3 + 5xy$

33a. binomial of degree 2
b. trinomial of degree 3
c. monomial of degree 6
d. binomial of degree 2
e. monomial of degree 3
f. trinomial of degree 4

34a. degree 4 ; $x^4 + 3x^2 - 4$
b. degree 3 ; $6x^3 - 5x - 9$
c. degree 4 ; $6x^4 - x^3 + 7x^2 - 4$
d. degree 4 ; $-2x^2y^2 + 10x^2y + 5y^2$
e. degree 4 ; $-x^4 + 3xy^2 - 4x^2$
f. degree 5 ; $a^2b^3 - 4a^3b - 2ab^2 + ab$
g. degree 5 ; $-x^3y^2 + 4xy^3 + 2x^2y$
h. degree 5 ; $m^2n^3 - 2n^4 + 3m^2n$
i. degree 5 ; $4x^2yz^2 - 2y^2z^2 + 3x^2y$

35. (Individual answers)
36a. false   b. true   c. false
d. false   e. true   f. false

4.2 Adding and Subtracting Polynomials

1a. $2x$; $2x^2y^3$ b. $2x$; $\frac{1}{4}x$
$-3x^2y$; $-3xy$ $-xy$; $-3xy$
$\frac{1}{4}y^3$; $\frac{1}{4}x$ $-3x^2y$; x^2y
$-xy$; $-x^2y^3$ $\frac{1}{4}y^3$; y^3
x^2y ; y^3 $2x^2y^3$; $-x^2y^3$

2-7. (Individual examples)
2. x ; $3x$ 3. $2y$; $-5y$ 4. $10a^2$; $-a^2$
5. $3m^2n$; m^2n 6. $4x^2y$; $-x^2y$ 7. 16 ; -5
8. $6x$; 6 9. $-12y$; -12 10. $30x^2$; 30
11. $-14y^2$; -14 12. $2x^2y$; 2 13. $9x^2$; 9
14. $9x^4y^2$; 9 15. $-x^6y^6$; -1
16. $9x$ 17. $3x$ 18. $7y$ 19. $-6y$
20. $3x^2$ 21. $2x^2$ 22. $-3x^2$ 23. $-6y$
24. 0 25. $-y$ 26. $3x^2$ 27. 0
28. $9xy$ 29. $-2xy$ 30. $3xy^2$ 31. $-2x^2y$
32. $6xy^2$ 33. 0
34. $= x^4 + 2x^4 = 3x^4$ 35. $= -2x^3 + x^3 = -x^3$
36. $= x^6 + 2x^6 = 3x^6$ 37. $= -4x^2 + 3x^2 = -x^2$

38. $= 9x^2 - 4x^2 = 5x^2$ 39. $= 4x^4 - x^4 = 3x^4$
40. $= 3x + 1 - x = 2x + 1$
41. $= -x^2 - 3x^2 + 5 = -4x^2 + 5$
42. $= 3x - 4x - 2 = -x - 2$
43. $= -2y + 5 + 2y = 5$
44. $= -x - 3 + 2 - 6x = -7x - 1$
45. $= x^2 + x^2 - 5 = 2x^2 - 5$
46. $= -y - 4 - 4y + 2 = -5y - 2$
47. $= x^3 - 4 + 2 - x^3 - 5x^3 = -5x^3 - 2$
48. $= 2x - x + 3y + 2y = x + 5y$
49. $= -7x - x - 4y + 6y = -8x + 2y$
50. $= -x + 6x + 8 - 10 = 5x - 2$
51. $= 6x^2 - 4x^2 + x + 2x = 2x^2 + 3x$
52. $= 2x + x - 3y - 4y = 3x - 7y$
53. $= 5x - 2x - y + 3y = 3x + 2y$
54. $= 3x + 2x - 2 - 8 = 5x - 10$
55. $= -4x - 6x - 5 - 3 = -10x - 8$
56. $= xy - 5xy + 5y + y = -4xy + 6y$
57. $= x^2 - 3x^2 + 2x - 4x = -2x^2 - 2x$
58. $= 4x^2 - x^2 - 3x - 2x = 3x^2 - 5x$
59. $= x^2y - x^2y + y + y = 2y$
60. $= -y^2 + y^2 - 4xy + xy = -3xy$
61. $= 7y^2 - y^2 - 2y + 1 = 6y^2 - 2y + 1$
62. $= -x^2 + 7x - 2x - 1 = -x^2 + 5x - 1$
63. $= x^2 + 2xy - 4xy + x = x^2 - 2xy + x$
64. $= -2x^2y + 3x^2 - y + y = -2x^2y + 3x^2$
65. $= 2x^2 + x^2 + x + 3x - 1 + 5 = 3x^2 + 4x + 4$
66. $= x^2 - 3x^2 + 4x - x - 5 + 2 = -2x^2 + 3x - 3$
67. $= 2x^2 + x^2 - xy + 3xy + y^2 - 2y^2 = 3x^2 + 2xy - y^2$
68. $= 3x^2 - x^2 + xy + xy - 2y^2 + y^2 = 2x^2 + 2xy - y^2$
69. $= 2x^2 - 3x^2 - 6x - 4x + 5 - 2 = -x^2 - 10x + 3$
70. $2x + 3$ 71. $7x + 2$
$x^2 + 4x$ $3x^2 - 4x$
$x^2 + 6x - 5$ $-2x^2 - x + 5$
$3x^2 - 4x + 5$ $4x^2 + 5x + 5$
72a. 2 b. -3 c. $\frac{1}{2}$ d. 10
e. 30 f. 5 g. 9 h. 36
73a. $-5x, 2.2x, -x$ b. $-2xy^2, 0.1xy^2, 4xy^2$
c. $2y^3, -y^3, 10y^3$ d. $-6xy, 3xy, 0.3xy$
e. $xy^3, -5xy^3, \frac{1}{3}xy^3$ f. $-1.25x^2y^2, (-xy)^2, 3(xy)^2$
74a. $2x + y$ b. $6x^2 + x$
c. $-4x^2 - 9y$ d. $17y^2 - 5xy$
e. $7x^2 + 3x - 2$ f. $-x^3 + 2x - 2y + 3$
g. $-x^2y - x^2 + 6$ h. $-2xy + 6x + 3y$
i. $-5xy^2 + 8xy - 2$ j. $-9xy + 4x - 6y - 5$
75a. false   b. false   c. true   d. true
76a. $5x + 40$ b. $7x + 55$ c. $2x + 15$
d. The difference is $31.

Answers

4.3 Multiplying Polynomials

1. x ; 1 ; $3x$; 3
2. x ; 4 ; $2x$; 8
3. $3x$; 1 ; $15x$; 5
4. $2x$; 3 ; $2x^2$; $3x$
5. x ; 6 ; x^2 ; $6x$
6. $4x$; 3 ; $4x^2$; $3x$
7. $= 5x - 10$
8. $= 12x + 2$
9. $= 2x - 8$
10. $= -3x + 3$
11. $= 2x^2 + 5x$
12. $= x^2 - 7x$
13. $= 3x^2 + 3x$
14. $= -x^2 - 10x$
15. $= 2x^2 + 10x$
16. $= -x^3 + 5x^2$
17. $= 6x^2 + 2x$
18. $= 2x^3 - 3x^2$
19. $= 8x^2 - 4x$
20. $= -12x^2 - 3x$
21. $= 2x^4 + 6x^2 - 8x$
22. $= 3x^3 - 6x^2 - 9x$
23. $= 4x^2 + 4x + 4x^3 = 4x^3 + 4x^2 + 4x$
24. $= -30x + 5x^4 - 10x^2 = 5x^4 - 10x^2 - 30x$
25. $= -x^3 - 4x^2 + x^4 = x^4 - x^3 - 4x^2$
26. $= -2x^4 + 2x^2 - 4x^3 = -2x^4 - 4x^3 + 2x^2$
27. $= 9x^4 - 12x^2 + 3x^3 = 9x^4 + 3x^3 - 12x^2$
28. $= -4x^2 + 4x^3 - 12x^4 = -12x^4 + 4x^3 - 4x^2$
29. $= 4x^4 - 2x^3 + 2x^5 = 2x^5 + 4x^4 - 2x^3$
30. $= -9x^4 + 15x^3 - 3x^5 = -3x^5 - 9x^4 + 15x^3$
31. a. 4   b. $2x$ c. $-x$ d. $2x^2$
32. a. $3x$; 4   b. $2x$; 6   c. $3x^2$; x ; 3
    d. $-2x^2$; $3x$; 5
33. $= 6x^3 + 3x^2$
    $6(-1)^3 + 3(-1)^2 = -6 + 3 = -3$
34. $= -2a^2 - 8a$
    $-2(5^2) - 8(5) = -2(25) - 40 = -50 - 40 = -90$
35. $= -6n^3 - n^2$
    $-6(3^3) - (3^2) = -6(27) - 9 = -162 - 9 = -171$
36. $= 3m^3 - 24m^2 + 3m$
    $3(-2)^3 - 24(-2)^2 + 3(-2) = 3(-8) - 24(4) - 6$
    $= -24 - 96 - 6 = -126$
37. $= 6k^3 + 6k^2 - 18k$
    $6(-3)^3 + 6(-3)^2 - 18(-3) = 6(-27) + 6(9) + 54$
    $= -162 + 54 + 54 = -54$
38. $= 4u^5 - 6u^3 - 8u^2$
    $4(2^5) - 6(2^3) - 8(2^2) = 4(32) - 6(8) - 8(4)$
    $= 128 - 48 - 32 = 48$
39. a. Perimeter: x ; $x + 3$; $4x + 6$
    Area: x ; $x + 3$; $x^2 + 3x$
    b. Perimeter: $4(6) + 6$; 30
    Area: $(6^2) + 3(6)$; 54
40. a. Perimeter: $2(x + 4 + 2x) = 6x + 8$
    Area: $(x + 4)(2x) = 2x^2 + 8x$
    b. Perimeter: $6(5) + 8 = 38$
    Area: $2(5^2) + 8(5) = 90$
41. a. $2(x - 2 + x) = 4x - 4$
    b. $4(5) - 4 = 20 - 4 = 16$
    She needs 16 m of fencing.

42. a. $x(x + 8) = x^2 + 8x$
    b. $20(x^2 + 8x) = 20x^2 + 160x$
43. a. $6(x)(3x + 1) = 18x^2 + 6x$
    b. $18(4^2) + 6(4) = 18(16) + 24 = 288 + 24 = 312$
    312 cm^2 of wood was used.
44. a. $5x - 5$ b. $-12y - 18$
    c. $7p^2 + 3p$ d. $-b^2 - 10b$
    e. $3n^2 + 24n$ f. $-12t^2 + 6t$
    g. $20a^3 - 6a^2$ h. $-s^5 + 2s^3 - s^2$
    i. $m^5 - 5m^4 + 2m^3$ j. $-24u^4 + 16u^3 + 8u$
    k. $-4g^5 + 12g^4 + 36g^2$ l. $15v^4 - 3v^3 - 30v^2$
    m. $3x^4 - x^2y - 2x^2$ n. $-3a^5b + 2a^2b^2 - ab^3$
45. a. $2x^2 + 3x$; 27   b. $2x^2 - 10x$; -12
    c. $-10y^2 - 5y$; -30   d. $-x^3 + 2x^2 - x$; -12
    e. $3y^4 - 12y^3 + 15y^2$; 204
    f. $-4x^4 + 12x^3 - 16x^2$; -144
46. a. Square:
    Perimeter = $8x$; Area = $4x^2$
    Rectangle:
    Perimeter = $16x + 4$; Area = $15x^2 + 6x$
    Parallelogram:
    Perimeter = $14x - 10$; Area = $8x^2 - 6x$
    b. The perimeter is 32 cm and the area is 54 cm^2.
    c. The lengths of any shape's sides must always be positive. The sides of the parallelogram have additional restrictions since they involve subtraction. $(4x - 3)$ and $(3x - 2)$ must be greater than 0, so x must be greater than $\frac{3}{4}$ and $\frac{2}{3}$ respectively. Therefore, x can be smaller than 1 cm as long as it is greater than $\frac{2}{3}$ cm.
47. a. $-x^2 + 30x$
    b. The total cost is $200 for 10 attendees.
    c. Total cost for 15 attendees: $225
    Total cost for 20 attendees: $200
    The total earned from 20 attendees would be less than the total earned from 15 attendees. Therefore, the owner should set a limit to 15 people to maximize profit.

4.4 Operations with Polynomials

1. 3 ; 3 ; 2 ; 2
   3 ; 2 ; 3 ; 4
   5 ; 7
2. $2x$; 1 ; x ; 5
   8 ; 3 ; 4 ; 15
   5 ; 11
3. x ; x ; $2x$; $2x$
   2 ; 2 ; 3 ; 6
   4 ; 3
4. x^2 ; x ; x ; 1
   5 ; 2 ; 5 ; 2
   3 ; 7

5. $= 4x + 20 + 12x - 6$
   $= 4x + 12x + 20 - 6$
   $= 16x + 14$
6. $= 16x + 56 - x^2 - 5x$
   $= -x^2 + 16x - 5x + 56$
   $= -x^2 + 11x + 56$
7. $= 3x^2 - 3x + 6x^2 + 2x$
   $= 3x^2 + 6x^2 - 3x + 2x$
   $= 9x^2 - x$
8. $= -10x^2 + 15x + 6x^2 + 48x$
   $= -10x^2 + 6x^2 + 15x + 48x$
   $= -4x^2 + 63x$
9. $= x^3 - 6x^2 + 10x + 8$
10. $= 4x^2 + 12x - 7x^3 - 2x^2$
    $= -7x^3 + 4x^2 - 2x^2 + 12x$
    $= -7x^3 + 2x^2 + 12x$
11. $= 6x^2 + 2x^3 - x^3 - 4x^2$
    $= 2x^3 - x^3 + 6x^2 - 4x^2$
    $= x^3 + 2x^2$
12. $= 18x^3 - 3x^2 - 2x^4 + 3x^3$
    $= -2x^4 + 18x^3 + 3x^3 - 3x^2$
    $= -2x^4 + 21x^3 - 3x^2$
13. $= -3x^3 - x^2 - 4x^2 + 24x$
    $= -3x^3 - 5x^2 + 24x$
14. $= -12x^3 + 6x^2 + 7x^3 - 7x$
    $= -12x^3 + 7x^3 + 6x^2 - 7x$
    $= -5x^3 + 6x^2 - 7x$
15. $= -7x^3 + 42x^2 - x^3 - 5x^2$
    $= -7x^3 - x^3 + 42x^2 - 5x^2$
    $= -8x^3 + 37x^2$
16. $= 8x^3 - 4x^2 + 6x^3 + 3x$
    $= 8x^3 + 6x^3 - 4x^2 + 3x$
    $= 14x^3 - 4x^2 + 3x$
17. $= 3x + 6 - 10x + 5 = -7x + 11$
    $-7(3) + 11 = -21 + 11 = -10$
18. $= 12x^2 - 4x + 6x + 6 = 12x^2 + 2x + 6$
    $12(1^2) + 2(1) + 6 = 20$
19. $= 2x^2 - 2x + 3x^2 + 6x = 5x^2 + 4x$
    $5(-1)^2 + 4(-1) = 5 - 4 = 1$
20. $= 3x^2 + 2x - 2x^2 - 10x = x^2 - 8x$
    $(-2)^2 - 8(-2) = 4 + 16 = 20$
21. $= 2x^3 + 10x^2 + 3x^3 - x^2 = 5x^3 + 9x^2$
    $5(5^3) + 9(5^2) = 5(125) + 9(25) = 850$
22. $= -2x^3 - 4x^2 + 4x^3 - 3x^2 = 2x^3 - 7x^2$
    $2(-3)^3 - 7(-3)^2 = 2(-27) - 7(9) = -117$
23. $= 3x^2 + x + 3x + 5 = 3x^2 + 4x + 5$
    $3(2^2) + 4(2) + 5 = 3(4) + 8 + 5 = 25$
24. $= 6x^2 + 4x - 2x + 3 = 6x^2 + 2x + 3$
    $6(-1)^2 + 2(-1) + 3 = 6 - 2 + 3 = 7$

25. B
    $= 30 + 10h + 30 + 10h$
    $= 20h + 60$
    $20(3) + 60 = 120$
    The total cost was $120.
26. A
    $= 1000 + 400d + 3600 + 450d$
    $= 850d + 4600$
    $850(14) + 4600 = 16\ 500$
    The total cost is $16 500.
27. A
    $= 2400m - 12\ 000 - 2250m + 7200$
    $= 150m - 4800$
    $150(35) - 4800 = 450$
    The difference in profit is $450 after 35 months.
28a. Portfolio A:
    $V = 3(3y + 220) + 5(4y + 180) + 5(7y + 140)$
    $\quad = 9y + 660 + 20y + 900 + 35y + 700$
    $\quad = 64y + 2260$
    Portfolio B:
    $V = 4(3y + 220) + 3(4y + 180) + 6(7y + 140)$
    $\quad = 12y + 880 + 12y + 540 + 42y + 840$
    $\quad = 66y + 2260$
  b. Portfolio A:
    $V = 64(5) + 2260$
    $\quad = 2580$
    Portfolio B:
    $V = 66(5) + 2260$
    $\quad = 2590$
    Portfolio A will have a value of $2580 and Portfolio B will have a value of $2590.
29a. Outer perimeter:
    $P = 2(8x + 5 + 12x)$
    $\quad = 2(20x + 5)$
    $\quad = 40x + 10$
    Area:
    $A = 12x(8x + 5) - (12x - 2x)(8x + 5 - 2x)$
    $\quad = 96x^2 + 60x - 10x(6x + 5)$
    $\quad = 96x^2 + 60x - 60x^2 - 50x$
    $\quad = 36x^2 + 10x$
  b. Outer perimeter:
    $P = 40(6) + 10$
    $\quad = 250$
    Area:
    $A = 36(6^2) + 10(6)$
    $\quad = 36(36) + 60$
    $\quad = 1356$
    The outer perimeter is 250 cm and the area is 1356 cm^2.

Answers

30a. $3x + 14$ b. $-x^2 + 10x$ c. $9x^2 - x$
  d. $2x^3 + 3x^2 - 20x + 16$ e. $-x^3 + 7x^2$
  f. $7x^3 + 3x^2 - 5x$ g. $3x^3 + 12x^2 - 27x + 18$
31a. $41a + 16$; 98   b. $b^2 + 28b$; -27
  c. $4a^2 - 3a$; 10   d. $-5b^2 - 3b + 6$; 4
  e. $a^3 - 6a^2 - 5a$; -26 f. $2b^3 + 10b^2 - 3b$; 11
32. Simplifying a polynomial expression can eliminate or reduce the number of variables in an expression. This then reduces the number of steps needed in substitution. It is less likely to compute large numbers when an expression is simplified.
33a. $C = 500 + 4.05c$ b. The cost is $8600.
34a. $C = 29x + 110y$ b. The cost is $10.37.

Quiz 4

  1. D   2. B   3. C   4. C
  5. C   6. D   7. C
  8a. $x^2 + 2x$; 2   b. $6y^2 + 4y - 3$; 2
  c. $-a^3 - 3a + 7$; 3 d. $8x^3 - 7x^2 + 6x - 4$; 3
  e. $-10c^3d + 6c^2 + 8cd + 12$; 4
  f. $-3i^2j^2 + 5i^3 + 2i^2j - ij$; 4
  9. $= 3a + 2a + 1 - 2 = 5a - 1$
  10. $= 3x - 2x + 4 - 2 = x + 2$
  11. $= x^2 + 2x^2 + 3x - 4x - 4 = 3x^2 - x - 4$
  12. $= 2y^2 - 3y^2 - 4y - 10 = -y^2 - 4y - 10$
  13. $= 12x^2 + 6x$ 14. $= 2a^2 - 10a$
  15. $= 3y^2 - 6y$ 16. $= 2x^3 - 6x^2 + 2x$
  17. $= 12x - 4 + 4x + 10 = 16x + 6$
  18. $= 0.8x + 4 + 6x^2 + 2x = 6x^2 + 2.8x + 4$
  19. $= 2a^3 + 4a^2 - 2a + a^3 - a^2 = 3a^3 + 3a^2 - 2a$
  20. $= 2n^2 + n - 6n^3 + 4n^2 = -6n^3 + 6n^2 + n$
  21. 5
    $15(-1) + 10 = -5$
  22. $2x$
    $2(-1)^3 - 8(-1)^2 + 6(-1) = -2 - 8 - 6 = -16$
  23. $-8x$
    $16(-1)^3 - 24(-1)^2 + 8(-1) = -16 - 24 - 8 = -48$
  24. $4x^2$
    $-4(-1)^4 - 8(-1)^3 + 16(-1)^2 = -4 + 8 + 16 = 20$
  25. $-5x$
    $-15(-1)^3 + 10(-1)^2 - 50(-1) = 15 + 10 + 50 = 75$
  26. $-6x^2$
    $12(-1)^3 + 72(-1)^2 = -12 + 72 = 60$

27.

Perimeter	Area
$4(3xy)$ $= 12xy$	$(3xy)^2$ $= 9x^2y^2$
$2(6x - 7 + 2x)$ $= 2(8x - 7)$ $= 16x - 14$	$2x(6x - 7)$ $= 12x^2 - 14x$
$2(5x - 3 + 3x + 6)$ $= 2(8x + 3)$ $= 16x + 6$	$4x(3x + 6)$ $= 12x^2 + 24x$
$(x + 3) + (3x - 1) + 2(2x + 3)$ $= 4x + 2 + 4x + 6$ $= 8x + 8$	$(x + 3 + 3x - 1)(2x) \div 2$ $= (4x + 2)x$ $= 4x^2 + 2x$

28a. $C = 50 + 10t + 35 + 8t$
    $= 85 + 18t$
  b. $t = 3$
    $C = 85 + 18(3)$
    $= 139$
    The total cost is $139.
29a. $C = 4(12d + 21)$ b. $d = 12$
    $= 48d + 84$ $C = 48(12) + 84$
        $= 660$
        The total cost is $660.
30a. $S = 4(6000 - 300y) + 9(3000 - 500y)$
    $= 24\,000 - 1200y + 27\,000 - 4500y$
    $= 51\,000 - 5700y$
  b. $y = 4$
    $S = 51\,000 - 5700(4)$
    $= 28\,200$
    The remaining donations after 4 years is $28 200.
  31. The degree of a polynomial is the highest degree among the terms that the polynomial is composed of.
  32. Yes, he is correct. A monomial can contain multiple variables or just a constant, as long as there is only 1 term in the expression.
    e.g. x^2, xyz, and -10 are all monomials.
  33. Either all three terms are like terms and can be simplified into a monomial, or two of the three terms are like terms and cancel each other out.
    e.g. $3x + 2x + x = 6x$
      $3x + (-3x) + 5 = 5$
  34a. $\frac{1}{2}y$
    b. $2a^2 - 9a + 0.1$
    c. $3x - 5$

35a. $= x(2x + 1) + 3(2x + 1)$
$\quad = 2x^2 + x + 6x + 3$
$\quad = 2x^2 + 7x + 3$
b. $= y(3y - 2) + 1(3y - 2)$
$\quad = 3y^2 - 2y + 3y - 2$
$\quad = 3y^2 + y - 2$
36. Let q be the number of quarters.
$\quad V = 0.25q + 0.1(25 - q)$
$\quad\quad = 0.25q + 2.5 - 0.1q$
$\quad\quad = 0.15q + 2.5$
$\quad 5.05 = 0.15q + 2.5$
$\quad 2.55 = 0.15q$
$\quad\quad q = 17$
Dimes: $25 - q = 25 - 17 = 8$
There are 17 quarters and 8 dimes.

Final Test

1. C   2. D   3. C   4. A
5. A   6. C   7. C
8. $= 5\sqrt{5} \times \sqrt{2} \div \sqrt{2} = 5\sqrt{5}$
9. $= 9 \times 2 = 18$
10. $= 3.5 \div 7 \times 10^2 \div 10^{-1} = 0.5 \times 10^3 = 500$
11. $= 3^{-1 + 3 - 2} = 3^0 = 1$
12. $= 7^4 \times 7^6 = 7^{4 + 6} = 7^{10}$
13. $= 10^2 \div 10^2 \times 10^{-3} = 10^{2 - 2 + (-3)} = 10^{-3}$
14. $= \dfrac{x^2}{y}$
15. $= a^2 b^2 (a^{-1}) = ab^2$
16. $= (2xy^2)(3xy) = 6x^2y^3$
17. $= 2n(n^{-6}) = 2n^{-5}$
18. $= -i^2(2i^2) = -2i^4$
19. $= 2a(\dfrac{a}{3}) = \dfrac{2}{3}a^2$
20a. $= 6x + 5x + 4 - 2 = 11x + 2$
$\quad 11(2) + 2 = 24$
b. $= 4x + 4 + 2x = 6x + 4$
$\quad 6(2) + 4 = 16$
21a. $= 5y - 20 + 2y - 4 = 7y - 24$
$\quad 7(-3) - 24 = -45$
b. $= 2y^2 + 10y + 3y^2 + 3y = 5y^2 + 13y$
$\quad 5(-3)^2 + 13(-3) = 5(9) - 39 = 45 - 39 = 6$
22. $\dfrac{4}{7}x = 12$
$\quad x = 12 \div \dfrac{4}{7}$
$\quad x = 21$
23. $x - 6 = -7$
$\quad x = -1$
24. $2x = 8 \times 7$
$\quad 2x = 56$
$\quad x = 28$

25. $2(3x + 1) = 4$
$\quad 3x + 1 = 2$
$\quad\quad 3x = 1$
$\quad\quad x = \dfrac{1}{3}$
26. $-3\sqrt{x} = -3$
$\quad \sqrt{x} = 1$
$\quad\quad x = 1$
27. $4x - 2x = -11 - 5$
$\quad\quad 2x = -16$
$\quad\quad x = -8$
28. T   29. F   30. F   31. T
32. F   33. T
34. $8.164 \times 10^6 \div 52$
$\quad = 8.164 \div 52 \times 10^6$
$\quad = 0.157 \times 10^6$
$\quad = 1.57 \times 10^5$
Its weekly revenue was 1.57×10^5.
35. Let x be the number of cups of flour to be added.
$\quad \dfrac{2}{5} = \dfrac{5}{8 + x}$
$\quad 2(8 + x) = 5 \times 5$
$\quad 16 + 2x = 25$
$\quad\quad 2x = 9$
$\quad\quad x = 4\dfrac{1}{2}$
She needs to add $4\dfrac{1}{2}$ more cups of flour.
36. $\quad 3\sqrt{15} \times 2 \div 2\sqrt{5}$
$\quad = 3\sqrt{3} \times \sqrt{5} \times 2 \div 2\sqrt{5}$
$\quad = 3\sqrt{3}$
The height is $3\sqrt{3}$ cm.
37. Let d be the number of dimes.
$\quad 0.25(25) + 0.1d = 8.35$
$\quad\quad 6.25 + 0.1d = 8.35$
$\quad\quad\quad 0.1d = 2.1$
$\quad\quad\quad\quad d = 21$
There are 21 dimes.
38. Let c be the capacity of the ladle.
$\quad \dfrac{5}{6}c + 50 = 175$
$\quad\quad \dfrac{5}{6}c = 125$
$\quad\quad\quad c = 125 \div \dfrac{5}{6}$
$\quad\quad\quad c = 150$
The capacity of the ladle is 150 mL.

Answers

39a. $S = m(600 - 20x + 850 - 25x)$
      $= m(1450 - 45x)$
      $= 1450m - 45mx$

  b. $S = 1450(6) - 45(6)(3)$
      $= 8700 - 810$
      $= 7890$
      They will save $7890 after 6 months.

40. $\sqrt{64}$ in simplest form is 8, which is a rational number. However, $\sqrt{23}$ cannot be simplified further and it cannot be expressed as a fraction of integers. So, $\sqrt{23}$ is not a rational number.

41. Yes, she is correct. A power with a positive base and a greater exponent means that the base is multiplied by itself more times, and thus is a greater number.

42. (Any 3 of the following with individual examples)
Product of Powers: $a^m \times a^n = a^{m+n}$
Quotient of Powers: $a^m \div a^n = a^{m-n}$
Power of a Power: $(a^m)^n = a^{mn}$
Negative Exponent: $a^{-p} = \dfrac{1}{a^p}$
Identity Exponent: $a^1 = a$
Zero Exponent: $a^0 = 1$

43. The sum of two trinomials results in a binomial when there are like terms in the trinomials of the opposite signs that can cancel each other out.
e.g. $(3x^2 + x + 1) + (x^3 - x - 1) = x^3 + 3x^2$
    $(x^2 + 2x + 1) + (-x^2 + x + 3) = 3x + 4$

44a. $\sqrt{8x} \times \sqrt{2x} = 2 \times 4$
    $\sqrt{16x^2} = 8$
      $4x = 8$
       $x = 2$

  b. $(3\sqrt{7})^2 = (\sqrt{x^3 - 1})^2$
    $9 \times 7 = x^3 - 1$
      $63 = x^3 - 1$
      $x^3 = 64$
      $x^3 = 4^3$
       $x = 4$

45a. $2y$
  b. $-2a - b + 3$

46a. Volume:
$V = s^3$
$8x^3 = s^3$
$2^3 x^3 = s^3$
$(2x)^3 = s^3$
$s = 2x$
The side length of the cube is $2x$.
Surface area:
$6s^2$
$= 6(2x)^2$
$= 6(4x^2)$
$= 24x^2$
The surface area is $24x^2$.

  b. Area:
$A = s^2$
$20x^4 = s^2$
$(\sqrt{20})^2(x^2)^2 = s^2$
$(\sqrt{20}x^2)^2 = s^2$
$s = \sqrt{20}x^2$
$s = 2\sqrt{5}x^2$
The side length of the square is $2\sqrt{5}x^2$.
Perimeter:
$4(2\sqrt{5}x^2)$
$= 8\sqrt{5}x^2$
The perimeter is $8\sqrt{5}x^2$.

47. Let d be the number of dimes.
$0.25(2d) + 0.1d + 0.05(430 - d - 2d) = 53$
$0.5d + 0.1d + 0.05(430 - 3d) = 53$
$0.6d + 21.5 - 0.15d = 53$
$0.45d = 31.5$
$d = 70$

Quarters: $2d = 2 \times 70 = 140$
Nickels: $430 - d - 2d = 430 - 140 - 70 = 220$
There are 140 quarters, 70 dimes, and 220 nickels.